Paul

Conversations with Jesus

from St John's Gospel

With study guide

Patrick Whitworth

ReSource

ReSource – helping to build a church which is diverse, local, renewed in the Spirit and effective in mission

Published by:
ReSource
13 Sadler Street, Wells, Somerset BA5 2RR
office@resource-arm.net
www.resource-arm.net
Charity no. 327035

ISBN 978-1-906363-39-0

Image acknowledgements

Cover photo & p28 : Fresco from Agios Gregoriou, Mount Athos
© Patrick Whitworth
p7 John the Evangelist, by Guido Reni, 1575-1642, public domain
p13 The Wedding at Cana © Fr Jerome Sanderson
p21 Christ instructing Nicodemus, by Crijn Hendricksz Volmarijn,
1601-1645, public domain
p35 Woman caught in adultery, from the original watercolour
© John Martin Borg
p41 Christ with Mary and Martha, Johannes Vermeer, 1632-1675, public domain
p49 Christ in the Wilderness, by Stanley Spencer © The Estate of Stanley Spencer
2013. All rights reserved DACS
p57 Jesus alone with Pilate, by William Hole, 1846-1917, public domain
p 65 Christ and Mary (detail), by Rembrandt Van Rijn, 1606-69, public domain
p 72 Christ with St Peter on the Sea of Galilee (detail) by Lucas Gassel,
1490-1568, public domain

Cover design by Wayne McMaster

Printed by Flexpress, 6 Coal Cart Rd, Birstall, Leicester LE4 3BY

Contents

Introduction

This book is designed to introduce ten conversations between Jesus and individuals encountered in St John's gospel – although the first conversation and one other are, as you will see, a little different from the rest. Several of these reflections were first given as talks at a house-party at Arisaig on the West Coast of Scotland in 2012, and I am grateful for the encouragement from all those who were there to publish them, and also for that special week of refreshment, teaching and renewal.

These ten studies are designed to be used in group discussion, with the purpose of discovering how to become *conversationalists with a difference*. Conversations can change our perspectives on life, ourselves and our relationship with, and understanding of, God.

Conversation is an integral part of life. Can you imagine a life without it? How awful it would be, unless you have a clear call to be a Trappist monk! In our society, with its members increasingly living alone, conversation is at a premium. For many, their main company is the television or the radio; the only conversation they might have is with the check-out assistant or a stranger at the bus stop. When my wife was away for a few days recently, I left the radio on for much of the time just to have some sound around the house. Others might have had music. Silence, with no conversation for hours on end, is a hard thing to bear. I am told that the rise in popularity of our café society is in part because people like to work in busy places, with their mobile phones or laptops to hand and a coffee not far away. I certainly enjoy that buzz in a café. Then again, conversation could be a dying art. Sometimes you see young adults seated around a table in a café, not speaking to each other at all. They have mobile phones out and, without lifting their heads, are busy sending texts, or surfing the net for some elusive piece of information, and not a word is spoken to the person across the table! Recently I heard the story of a mother telling her teenage children of a new social media that had just been launched. 'What is it?' they eagerly asked, mystified that their *mother* should know anything about it, but still hoping to add it to their increasing number of social media possibilities. 'Conversation!!' she replied.

In many households, family meals have become a thing of the past, yet conversation is one of the great pleasures of life, along with reading, sitting in front of a fire, walking, playing sport or going to a film or concert. Jesus was undoubtedly a great conversationalist: perceptive, versatile, able to tell riveting stories, topical, well informed, controversial, provocative at times, and not afraid to raise a loaded subject. And all the while he seemed to know something his hearers didn't, which was intriguing, maybe slightly frightening, but never dull. In this series of studies we will watch him in action, making conversation with all kinds of people and sometimes in highly unusual and difficult circumstances. Indeed so unusual were some of these settings, we would have to say they were utterly unique.

Patrick Whitworth

All Saints Church, Bath Weston
July 2013

Study 1

Conversation with the world

John 1.1-16

This passage at the start of John's gospel represents a conversation with a difference. It is not a conversation with an individual as most of the others will be. It is, instead, the final and culminating stage of a conversation with the world.

It is a conversation that began with a man called Abraham, whom God spoke to one day in Mesopotamia (Genesis 12.2). God said, 'I will make you into a great nation and I will bless you: I will make your name great and you will be a blessing.' This was the beginning of a plan that God had formed for choosing a nation into which his Son, the Messiah, would one day be born. And it was a conversation necessitated by an earlier conversation that he had had with Adam and Eve in the Garden of Eden aeons before. God was in the habit of speaking with Adam and Eve in the cool of the evening, in an open leisurely kind of way (see Genesis 3.8). But on this occasion they were nowhere to be seen; they were hiding, they felt naked and ashamed, they were guilty, and they dreaded conversation with God. Hiding like naughty children from a parent, they crept from their shelter, covering themselves, in order to talk to God. The ensuing conversation showed it gave God no pleasure that they had disobeyed his command. Their paradise was at an end. They were banished from the garden. Adam would have to labour hard for his food, and Eve would labour in pain to bear children (Genesis 3). Worst of all, the fellowship with God was broken; previously friends, they were now more like enemies – or at the least, they were estranged – and the bacillus of sin had infected the human race.

A new conversation had to begin to repair the damage. God would choose a family, a nation, and later would choose servants like Moses along with prophets, priests and kings to serve him. The new conversation began with Abraham in Haran, which he left for Canaan (Genesis 12). Late one clear night, God promised Abraham descendants more numerous than the starry host above (Genesis 15), even though Abraham had no heir (Genesis 18). An heir was born, laughter was restored to the family and God's great project of preparing a nation for his Son was underway. This conversation continued with Jacob, through many twists and turns, and then through Moses, especially when God spoke to him face to face as a man talks to his friend (Exodus 33). But the trouble was that although God spoke, the people were rarely attentive and frequently, having heard him, ignored what had been said. But God did not give up speaking to those whom he chose and to those who would listen to him. The prophets were his spokesmen, and none more so than Isaiah or Jeremiah before the Exile, or Ezekiel during it. Some prophets had short pithy messages like Haggai, others much longer ones. Essentially they said 'return to your creator and redeemer, and live.' Often these messengers were imprisoned, isolated or even killed. Soon the time for the final, great conversation arrived; a conversation that would be conducted with the whole world, but which had its beginning in the most unusual of broadcasts.

8

The broadcaster in this case was the Apostle John, one of the sons of Zebedee, who had been called by Jesus in the very early stages of his ministry, together with James, his brother, and Peter, a fellow fisherman on Galilee (see Mark 1.14ff). These three formed the inner circle amongst the disciples, often privileged with special attention from Jesus. James was later killed in the persecution that came on the church (Acts 12.2). Peter, after spending time in Jerusalem and Antioch, moved to Rome around 63AD, where his memoirs formed the basis of Mark's gospel. John at some point left Jerusalem, and moved to Ephesus where he lived for many years as one of the leaders of the Ephesian church, well after it had been founded by the Apostle Paul in 57AD (see Acts 19). It was probably from here, as an old man, in c.90AD, during the reign of the Emperor Domitian, that he was exiled to the island of Patmos where he received his extraordinary revelation one Sunday (Revelation 1.10). And around that time, either before or after his exile, John composed and broadcast his own highly reflective gospel.

John's gospel was quite unlike the other three. It is probable he knew of the other gospels and determined to write a different one. His audience were Hellenised (Greek speaking) Jews who lived in the Diaspora (that is, in the cities of the Roman Empire scattered around the Eastern Mediterranean). They were influenced by the teaching of the Gnostics, who had a complex system of thought that denied Jesus had come in human flesh, since in their view no deity could mingle with what they regarded as dirty human flesh. They believed that what was needed was an illuminating experience of knowledge *(gnosis)* which would give an eternal destiny to its recipients. As such, the Gnostics opposed the idea of Incarnation and the teaching that through faith in Jesus we may obtain eternal life. John determined to refute their erroneous thinking and show that the Word became Flesh, and that through faith in him we may receive eternal life. He therefore wrote his gospel in a different way. As the early church Father, Clement of Alexandria, wrote 'Last of all John, perceiving that the external facts had been made plain in the gospels, being urged by friends and inspired by the Spirit, composed a spiritual gospel'.[1] What

---

[1] Patrick Whitworth: *The Word from the Throne*, p.17.

he wrote was a gospel of deep theological reflection composed around seven signs and seven great *I am* sayings, in a threefold construction: the revelation of Jesus to the World (Chs 1-11), the revelation of Jesus to his disciples (Chs 13-17) and the glorification of the Word for the world (Chs 18-21). The stated aim was that the reader might believe and have *life* (20.31). John composed his gospel using a mix of narrative, sign, symbol, saying and discourse, which including fierce debates with the Jews, protracted teaching as in the Upper Room, and the conversations which we shall be studying.

Before the gospel gets underway, there is a prologue (as there is an epilogue at the end in John 21) in which the great themes of the gospel are introduced. This is our conversation with the world.

The prologue is rather like an overture at the beginning of a symphony. Just as in an overture many of the musical phrases which will resonate through the symphony are stated or played at the outset, so in the prologue of St John's gospel the themes and words which will be developed through the ministry of Jesus are set out in a piece of theological writing about the Incarnation and the ministry of Christ which is beyond compare. The words and ideas cascade through the prologue: words like life, light and darkness, the world, receive, believe, birth, children, flesh, grace, truth and finally glory. Each of these burst one after another in a theological fireworks display. Later in the gospel we shall see grace and truth at work in the conversations with the woman caught in adultery and the Samaritan woman (John 8 and 4). Light can be seen as the central motif in the conversation with the man born blind (John 9). Glory will be revealed at the Wedding at Cana of Galilee and supremely in the Cross (John 2 and 12.23ff). Birth will be the chief metaphor in the conversation with Nicodemus. Truth and its meaning will be central to the conversation with Pilate (John 18 & 19). Grace will be the underlying theme in the restoration of Peter on the shore of Galilee (John 21) and the theme of the world will appear and reappear throughout the gospel – notably in John 3.16-17. So in a few short sentences all these themes will be introduced and later revisited through the narrative of the gospel. And the purpose of all this was to demonstrate so powerfully that Jesus was the Christ, so that through belief in him we might have life. *Life* is another seminal word in the gospel, for it is what we are given as a consequence of believing: God's life, eternal life, life that consists in knowing both the Father and the Son – see John 17.3 – life in all its fullness. As Jesus famously said in one of his discourses, 'I have come that they may have life, and have it to the full' (10.10).

So the prologue is like an overture. It anticipates what is to come and drives up our expectation for what is to follow. But at its centre is the Word taking on flesh: here is the central idea and the dynamic heart of the passage. The word, in Greek *the logos*, took on flesh or, as it is in Greek, *sarx*. John declares, 'The word became flesh and dwelt among us' (literally *tabernacled* among us). The word *logos* was obviously known to the Greeks long before the Apostle John used it, but as a description of Jesus it is unique to John's writing. The Word reappears in Revelation 19.13 where we see the Word of God in combat against his enemies. He is the Rider on a White Horse also called Faithful and True.

The meaning of *logos* in Greek philosophy came principally from Zeno, a Stoic philosopher from Cyprus in 313BC. It meant the principle of reason that came from god which gave significance, coherence and meaning to creation. So for the Stoics 'god infused creation with logos'.[2] It was a term further recycled by an influential thinker called Philo, who taught in the Alexandrian philosophical schools in the early 1st century (20BC-50AD). Philo was a Jewish philosopher working in Greek, but familiar with Hebrew. He used the word *logos* to describe the wisdom and expression of God. Some forty years later, John, writing in nearby Ephesus, chose the same word to describe the second person of the Trinity leaving the glory of heaven to taken on human flesh; thus the Word became Flesh (1.14a). For John it denoted the pre-existent Christ who dwelt eternally with the Father, becoming God in human form, no less than the Father but distinct from him and obedient to him: come to redeem and give life. Thus one of our conversations in this series must be a conversation with the Father (John 17), since this gospel draws back the curtain on the relationship of Jesus, the Word made flesh, with his Father, like no other.

---

[2] *The Word from the Throne*, p. 99

The prologue introduces the themes of the gospel, but pre-eminently the chief theme, which is that the pre-existent, all creating, all powerful Son of God, described by John as the Word, has entered our world of mess and sin. He came to bring life, light, truth and grace, and what we shall be treated to throughout the gospel, and especially in these conversations, is a demonstration of how that life was displayed by Jesus, how people may be born into that new life (1.12-13), and how in the later stages of the gospel, that glory will be revealed for all to see (12.23-33).

It is time to consider together the nature of this conversation with the world.

Study Questions

What is the purpose of the prologue of St John's gospel?

What are the main themes of the prologue?

What themes do you especially like in the prologue? What for you are key words in the prologue and why?

What does the prologue tell us about Jesus, before and after his Incarnation?

In what sense do you think this could be called the conclusion of a conversation with the world?

What do you especially like about this opening of the conversation?

What do you think that the world today especially needs to hear from the prologue?

What part do you think you have in helping the world hear the message contained in the prologue?

Summarise.

Study 2

Jesus' Conversation with his mother during the wedding at Cana of Galilee

John 2.1-11

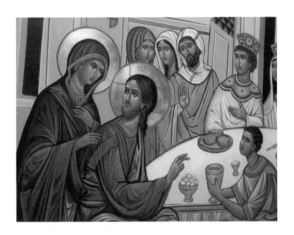

Jesus' conversation with his mother took place at the wedding at Cana of Galilee. When Jesus arrived with his disciples, Jesus' mother was already there (2.1). We can safely assume that the wedding was of either close friends of Jesus' family, or maybe even relatives. Cana is not far from Nazareth and the families could have seen much of each other. It could be for this reason, that is, their familiarity with her, that the organisers or servants informed Mary of the problem they faced before it became evident or public, so that something could be done. It is possible that they had some inkling Jesus might be able to help, although since this was to be his first miracle, there was no precedent in his life for anything like this.

Weddings in those days lasted the best part of a week and they involved most of the village. Weddings often began on a Wednesday if the couple were being married for the first time. The marriage of widows or widowers, or a second wedding, took place on a Thursday (sivorce under some Jewish rabbinic matrimonial laws was comparatively easy).[3] The bridegroom normally collected the bride from her family home, often arriving late at night. Hence the parable of the wise and foolish virgins (bridesmaids) had its origins in custom. In terms of the parable, the bridesmaids who had too little oil for their lamps went out to buy some more oil and in so doing missed the arrival of the bridegroom who came with his party late at night (Matthew 25.1-13). In the case of the parable, as no doubt in reality, 'the bridegroom was (often) a long time in coming.' Having collected the bride from her home, the party went back to the bridegroom's house for the wedding and the celebrations. Whether the celebrations continued for days without the bride and groom present we cannot be sure, but what we can be sure of is that the wedding was a family, community and public event. It is quite possible that this bridegroom's family ran out of wine quite early on in the proceedings.

So imagine the consternation, with several hundred guests to cater for and the wedding hardly underway, when the wine ran out! The servants would have been the first to notice. Going to the flagons where the wine was kept, they would have seen that the wine was almost finished. Someone came to Mary and told her that the party had no more wine. A major embarrassment was looming for the groom's family, one for which they would become infamous in the village. They would be seen as stingy, inefficient or lacking foresight. No father of the bride in our society would ever forget it if he ran out of wine at his daughter's wedding, and neither would the guests! It would always remain at very least an uncomfortable moment. But as with so much in John's gospel, the material is a symbol for the spiritual. What is true of bread, vines, doors, water and wind applies also to wine. They are all symbols of the life of God, the life of the Spirit and the richness of his presence. To run out of wine means something spiritually too – what could this signify?

---

[3] Eg in the writings of Hillel the Elder, a renowned rabbi contemporary with Jesus.

There are two levels in which the wine runs out: metaphorically or spiritually, and corporately and personally. As this was the first sign that Jesus performed in his ministry, it surely has significance not simply for the wedding guests present on that occasion, but indeed for the whole community of Israel. *In a spiritual but nonetheless real way their wine had also run out*. Israel's wine had run out. The Old Covenant had run its course. It was dry, empty and lifeless with no sparkle or hope or life-giving quality left. The Torah could never give life and the further it was enforced by the Pharisees, the more burdensome it became. It was time for the Law to be replaced by grace. As John says in his prologue, that overture to the gospel: 'For the law came through Moses: grace and truth came through Jesus Christ' (1.17). And as Jesus said to the teachers of the Law later in the gospel of John, 'You diligently study the scriptures because you think that by them you possess eternal life. These are the scriptures that testify about me, yet you refuse to come to me to have life' (5.39-40). Coming to him was the way to a new start in relationship with God; if you like, it was an opportunity to replenish and renew the wine that had run dry.

This may be the case for some in your group whose Bible study or discussion you lead. Everything may have been exhausted spiritually. It may seem that there is no more to give, resources have been drained and expended. It as though the cupboard is bare. What Mary said to Jesus, 'They have no more wine,' could be equally true for some in your group as well. It is time for re-filling.

Jesus' response to his mother's request for help is initially not very encouraging! He says 'Dear woman, why do you involve me? My time has not yet come'(John 2.4). This could be seen as a brush off, like Jesus' words to the Syro-Phoenican woman, when he said, 'It is not right to take the children's bread and toss it to their dogs' (Mark 7.27). What kind of response were such remarks supposed to elicit? Nevertheless, Mary was not put off. She gave this classic advice to the servants, 'Do whatever he tells you' (John 2.5). Although this was the beginning of Jesus' ministry and none of his great works had yet occurred, she knew well the potential of her son. Maybe she recalled the circumstances of his conception, the strange and wonderful events surrounding his birth, the visit of the awestruck shepherds and the star-gazing wise men, or his demeanour through almost thirty years of childhood and adult life. She had pondered all these things in her heart and was waiting for the fulfilment of the prophecy over him. Maybe she had an inkling that this moment would herald the destiny to which he had been called. Jesus had enigmatically said, 'My time has not yet come', but at the very least it was perhaps the end of the beginning, if not the beginning of the end. For Jesus, the phrase 'his time' seemed to be clearly related to the revelation of his glory principally on the cross (see 12.23). This hour or time may have not yet come, but with his Baptism behind him (1.29ff), his identification with his mission complete, and his equipping through the infilling of the Spirit accomplished, then surely its beginning was very close. Could it be that Jesus thought that if he performed this miracle, then the course of his destiny leading to the cross would be irreversibly set in motion?

John Calvin wrote: 'Whenever the Lord keeps us in suspense and delays his aid, it does not mean that he is inactive, but rather he regulates his work so that he acts only at the right time.' Timing therefore is of the essence of his activity.

'Do whatever he tells you,' Mary said – surely a piece of spiritual advice that never runs dry. What could God be telling members of your group to do? Is there time to listen to his voice and hear his instruction? How do we hear?

Jesus saw the six stone water-jars which the Jews kept for ceremonial washing in the house or nearby. They contained around 75-115 litres apiece – approximately 600 litres, therefore about 700 bottles of wine in total. 'It makes little difference whether we take him to mean that all the water in the stone pots had become wine, or only that which was drawn by the servants to supply what was needed.' The stone jars were filled with water and when the water was drawn it was exquisite wine.

What is the significance of this sign or miracle, what does it teach us? Firstly, it is worth pointing out two things: the extraordinary surprise of it, and the affirmation of marriage that it contains. Firstly, the surprise: if you didn't know from John that this was Jesus' first miracle, would you ever guess that for his first sign or miracle on earth Jesus would produce a prodigious amount of wine for an occasion where the guests had probably already drunk enough? What a surprising start to his ministry! You might expect a healing, a deliverance, or the provision of food for the hungry - all of which Jesus would perform often – but he started with this miracle. Why? Well, the miracle was indeed an affirmation of marriage itself and furthermore an illustration of the love God has for humankind, as described vividly both in the Song of Songs and in the final vision of Revelation (21.1-4), which pictures the wedding of the Lamb (the bridegroom) to the church (the bride). But there was more.

There is something underlying and more basic to the sign, which, if you think about it, is not so surprising. For if we are right to see this miracle as an illustration of God's new provision for his people, an indication that the Old Covenant based on Law was at an end and spent, and that a new covenant based on faith in his son was beginning (to be sealed with his sacrificial blood), then this sign is both a miracle in itself and a sign of this new abundant provision by God through his son. It is a sign of the generosity of God in starting a new covenant more lavish and extravagant than anything yet seen. It is typified by the quantity and quality of the wine produced. The Steward of the feast famously says to the bridegroom (in a nice piece of Johannine irony) 'Everyone brings out the choice wine first and then the cheaper wine after the guests have had too much to drink; but you have saved the best till now' (2.10). What was true of the wine was true of the generosity and provision of God: the New Covenant far surpassed the Old, Jesus far surpassed the messengers of the Old Covenant; the prophets; and the salvation procured by Jesus far surpassed what had been previously offered by the system of law and sacrifice. The age of the Spirit was dawning and the age of the letter was past. In a word, the Kingdom had arrived and the king was here. No wonder it was therefore the first sign, and more than anything else it brought joy to a tired and jaded Israel. Joy was surely the outcome of such provision, and the touchstone of Jesus' presence.

Finally, John makes the first of many editorial comments in his gospel, that in this, the first of his signs (there are seven in all), Jesus revealed his *glory* – a telling word in the gospel. God's glory is the revelation of his character to a watching and waiting world. One can only imagine Mary's smile when she saw the outcome of her intervention – 'They have no more wine' and her advice to the anxious caterers to 'do whatever he tells you.' She must have thought that the fulfilment of Gabriel's promise that she would bear 'the Son of the Most High' (Luke 1.32) had begun. And it is a nice touch that it was the servants who knew the reality of what has happened. After all, they filled the jars with water and drew off the wine. They too must have smiled when the guests were surprised at the quality of the wine and their glasses were filled *again and again* by attentive servants. The servants were in on the miracle joke! And should not we his servants be both surprised and delighted to see the joy that God's grace brings and the glory that shines around, and likewise put our faith in him?

Study Questions

What do you think is the significance of this miracle or sign?

What does this sign teach us about Mary and her regard for Jesus?

In what ways does Mary's comment 'they have no more wine' resonate with us and our lives?

What do you think Mary expected her son to do when she said to the servants 'does whatever he tells you?'

What does this miracle tell us about what Jesus has come to do?

In what ways does Jesus, so to speak, turn water into wine now? Any examples?

What do you think the servants learn in the story? In what ways do we resemble the servants?

It may be that some in your group feel that they **have run out of wine** *for whatever reason, so be ready to gather round and pray especially for them during or at the end of the study.*

Study 3

A Conversation with Nicodemus, a ruler of the Jews

John 3.1-21

In the opening sentence of this story we are told two things about Nicodemus: he is a Pharisee and he is a ruler of the Jews. Among the population of Jerusalem, indeed in Israel, he is one of the elite. As a Pharisee, he is a part of a movement that stretched back for about 170 years before the ministry of Jesus. The group known as the Pharisees came into being as a movement of reform and purity in Israel, distinct from the Hellenising influence of the Greeks and the pagan influence of both Greeks and Romans whose presence was then being felt. Pharisaism began during the Hasmonean dynasty of Greek rulers. It marked a return to the strict observance of the Law or Torah, and as such represented a kind of resistance movement to paganism and its effects in Israel. Pharisees were originally called Hasidists and set out to follow the teaching and example of Ezra, who instructed the Israelites after their return from exile. Their object was to prevent creeping religious syncretism in Israel, to resist paganism in all its forms, and to teach the law comprehensively.

However, in their zeal they turned Judaism into a wearisome burden and also fell into the trap of self-righteousness in regard to the law, something for which Jesus continually criticised them. They found 613 commands in the law to obey, of which 248 were negative and 365 positive (one for each day of the year!) They also codified 39 prohibitions of what *not* to do on the Sabbath. It was in pressing these rules on the people that they made 'man for the Sabbath and not Sabbath for man.' In a word, they had lost the spiritual wood in the religious trees; they had replaced a vibrant relationship with *Yahweh* with a living burden of regulation (see Matthew 23 for Jesus' condemnation of their spirituality). Disciplined and very well taught in the Pharisaic schools in Jerusalem, they knew the Jewish scriptures intimately. Most if not all of the Pharisees in the Sanhedrin were also scribes and had studied the scriptures since boyhood. Nicodemus was one of these, but he was more.

He was also a ruler of the Jews, a member of the Sanhedrin - the Jewish Ruling council, which was upheld by the Romans to govern the people and as a ruling body to issue regulations. Nicodemus was then one of the 70 or so most influential citizens in Jerusalem, highly educated, articulate but also of enquiring mind; and this is what brought him one night to see Jesus. He was extremely circumspect and cautious in his approach.

His opening remarks seemed carefully crafted and well rehearsed in his mind - they strike me as a good example of diplomatic language or *foreign-office speak!* He is respectful, saying, 'Rabbi, we know you are a teacher who has come from God' (3.2). He recognises the authenticity of the miraculous signs that Jesus performed as God-given. But despite this respectful and well-intentioned opening gambit, he does not get a very indulgent response from Jesus. Indeed, far from it. Jesus' riposte or reply is almost brutally to the point. 'I tell you the truth, no one can see the kingdom of God unless he is born again' (3.3). Jesus uses a well-known metaphor, which goes to the heart of what he means, when he says: 'He must be born again'. It is a well chosen, pithy, extremely memorable, and famous phrase, although it is often used as a rather pejorative description of some Christians.

Why does Jesus use the metaphor of new birth or birth? And why in particular does he use it in conversation with a Pharisee? Why use metaphors at all, as Jesus frequently does in his conversations? It is worth thinking about, and while we are on the subject, why don't *we* use metaphors in describing faith in God and Christ to others? Presumably Jesus used this metaphor of birth for one principal reason: that is, if Nicodemus' whole spirituality or religion was predicated on self-effort, and his notion of acceptance by God based on obeying the law, then to speak of being born from above or being born again as the only way into the Kingdom points to something beyond all self-effort. After all, birth is something that happens mysteriously because the chemistry of mother and child desire it. For who can predict when exactly a birth will occur? Likewise, to enter or be birthed into the Kingdom of God is beyond human control.

For a moment, in response to Jesus' statement, Nicodemus thought that it was literally necessary to be born all over again to enter the Kingdom. He said almost laughingly, 'How can a man be born when he is old? Surely he cannot enter a second time into his mother's womb to be born?' (3.4) Just as physical birth is the necessary prelude to life, so this spiritual birth (or regeneration) is the necessary beginning of life in the Kingdom of God. Thus Jesus emphasises this new birth as something we simply cannot do ourselves.

He goes on to explain the process of birth, using another metaphor – of wind, this time – symbolising the Spirit. Realising that he needed to explain the process of this spiritual birth, Jesus described its occurrence in a classic piece of teaching. Entry into the Kingdom depends on water and Spirit. Water almost certainly depicts repentance. John the Baptist, as has already been shown in the gospel, used water as a symbol of repentance, cleansing and forgiveness (see John 1.26-27). But John also pointed to Jesus as the bringer of the Spirit following his death (see John 1.29,33). The spiritual birth which brings a person into the realm of the Kingdom comes through a double process: firstly, repentance, which the person does him or herself, and secondly, new birth which is done for them by the Spirit. Hence, entry into the Kingdom is by water and the Spirit, and this is the process referred to as being born from above or being born again. It is a double life, i.e. physical birth followed by a kingdom birth, and a double entry by water and the Spirit. Jesus puts it extremely clearly: 'Flesh gives birth to flesh, but the Spirit gives birth to Spirit' (3.7) – two realms, two dynamics, two perspectives – the flesh and the Spirit. After the flesh, the Spirit. But how does the Spirit work? Like wind!

In what ways is the Spirit like wind? Why is it such a good metaphor for the activity and person of the Spirit? Jesus explains the similarity between wind and Spirit: 'The wind blows wherever it pleases. You hear its sound, but you cannot tell where it comes from or where it is going' (3.8). So it is with everyone born of the Spirit. Some of the basic characteristics of wind are that it is invisible; you can feel it, hear it, watch its effects, but you can never see it! You can see trees bend, leaves scurry along the ground, waves lashed and stirred to foaming, windmills turn, ships move with full sails, but you never see the wind! You see its effects but never the wind itself. Likewise with the Spirit, you never see him but you see his working: change or transformation, the sense of God's presence, healing, tears, joy, repentance, love, mission, glory and awe. All these and others besides are the effects of his activity. But you can never see him: he is invisible. Like the wind, he too can be the gentle whisper, the pleasant breeze or the howling gale. He comes in many ways; there is a variety of working (see 1 Corinthians 12.4-6).

In 1987 there was a great gale in South Eastern England and millions of trees were uprooted. In South London it was as if a giant had come through the night uprooting trees and leaning them against houses, plucking them up as if with a great hand. It was the wind. On other days the wind can be just the faintest breeze. And it blows where it will. Who knows why the wind changes direction, veers and blows strong or weak? 'You cannot tell where it comes from or where it is going.' The very unpredictability of the wind is like the Spirit. You can never tell where he will blow next or whose life he will touch or turn upside down in a moment: a C S Lewis or a John Newton; a gang leader or heroin addict; a prisoner or a politician fallen on hard times, your boss or your neighbour; the chance encounter or the long-prayed for relative. Who knows where he, the Spirit, might blow.

Nicodemus was stunned: 'How can this be!' Pharisee and ruler of the people though he was, Nicodemus knew nothing of such things. Yes, he knew the Torah, its prohibitions, its regulations and its demands. But even though he was a teacher of Israel, he knew none of the spiritual principles of which Jesus spoke: the need for new birth, the work of the Spirit, the limits of the flesh to inherit eternal life (see 3.10). Jesus was tough on him: 'I have spoken to you of earthly things and you do not believe; how then will you believe if I speak of heavenly things?' (3.12) And then Jesus moved on one more stage in this riveting conversation: he talked about where the wind blows most powerfully, where new birth occurs especially, where a new beginning starts in this spiritual birth ward. It happens in knowing the Son of Man, but more especially it is in knowing and experiencing the message of the serpent. What serpent, and how the Son of Man is connected to the story of this serpent, we must look at next.

When the Israelites were wandering in the desert, as recorded in the book of Numbers, they fell once again into grumbling: 'Why have you brought us up out of Egypt to die in the desert? There is no bread! There is no water! And we detest this miserable food!' (Numbers 21.5-6). In judgement, snakes were sent into the camp, and many people were bitten and in danger of losing their lives. So Moses, having been told to do so by God, erected a bronze serpent on a pole and any who looked at the serpent on the pole were healed. Likewise Jesus said any who looked with faith on the Son of Man, who would be lifted up on the cross, would themselves live (John 3.14-15). Thus new birth or eternal life proceeds from faith in the Son of God who is to be lifted up like the serpent on the cross. The wind of the Spirit blows most strongly and powerfully from the cross. Jesus, the Son of God, became like a serpent to draw from us the poison from the bite of that great serpent, Satan. Or as Paul graphically puts it, 'God made him who had no sin to be sin for us, so that in him we might become the righteousness of God' (2 Corinthians 5.21). What an exchange: our poison for his righteousness!

Many people's lives have been poisoned by such things as bitterness, resentment, wrongdoing, regret or grave injustice, but this poison can be drawn by the Cross: forgiveness, hope, healing and an example of unjust suffering are to be found there, all of which can both restore and inspire.

Nicodemus must have gone away very thoughtful. We know by the end of the gospel he was a believer (John 19.39). John still calls him the man who had come by night, now he comes after the crucifixion *by day* to fetch and embalm the body of Jesus. 'He (Joseph of Arimathea) was accompanied by Nicodemus, the man who earlier had visited Jesus at night. Nicodemus brought a mixture of myrrh and aloes, about seventy-five pounds. Taking Jesus' body, the two of them wrapped it, with the spices, in strips of linen' (19.39-40). Did he realise that he had seen the fulfilment of Jesus' words and had witnessed him lifted up on the cross like the serpent in the wilderness? One imagines so.

The straight talking of Jesus to Nicodemus bore fruit. He believed. The teacher of Israel, the Scribe, the Pharisee and ruler of the people was born from above, through new birth and not observance of the Torah; through the wind of the Spirit and not the letter of the law; through the redemption of the cross and not through outward religious rituals. Nicodemus had spoken with the living Word, had handled the body of Christ, the crucified Word, and had presumably either seen himself or heard told the fact of the risen Word.

No wonder that in conclusion to this conversation John gives as editorial comment (rather than as part of the conversation) the summary that 'God so loved the world that he gave his one and only Son, that whoever believes in him shall not perish but have eternal life. For God did not send his Son into the world to condemn the world, but save the world through him' (3.16-17).

Study Questions

Why do you think Jesus was so straight and tough in his conversation with Nicodemus?

What do you think Nicodemus hoped to get out of the conversation?

What are the present day advantages and disadvantages of the metaphor of being 'born again'?

How does the event or process of being 'born again' take place?

Why is 'wind' such a good metaphor for the Spirit?

What do you think the relationship is between the Spirit and the Cross (the wind and the serpent)?

What kinds of things poison our lives, and how can we get rid of the poison?

In what state of mind and heart do you think Nicodemus left the conversation?

Are there any Nicodemuses around today? Who might they be? How would we engage them in conversation about faith?

Study 4

Conversation with the woman at the Well

John 4.1-42

Our next conversation could not be more different from the one between Jesus and Nicodemus, in terms of the individual involved, her character, or the setting. After all we don't even know the name of the person to whom Jesus was talking. She is simply known as the 'Woman at the Well.' Perhaps Jesus did not say her name, or maybe John was content to leave her anonymous, with the emphasis instead on the word derived from the setting of their meeting: the well, and the metaphor of their conversation arising from it – the water of life.

Whereas Nicodemus was a highly educated man, a scribe, a Pharisee, a Ruler of the Jews and member of the Sanhedrin, the governing body of Jerusalem, the woman at the well was a Samaritan, a woman of dubious morals as it turns out, who was perhaps forced by her lifestyle to come to the well at the hottest time of the day (4.6), at the sixth hour, because she was ostracised by others.

The well has its own history. Dug by Jacob perhaps some 1500 years before, it was still in use. Jacob had given the land around it to Joseph, the favourite son of Jacob, who was himself a kind of type or forerunner of Christ. This same Jacob was, after Abraham, the founder of the Jewish nation. He was named Israel (or struggler with God) after his night-time wrestling with God on his return to the Promised Land following his sojourn in Paddan-Aram (Genesis 32.22-32 and 35.10). This land, which was situated near the local town of Sychar, was in Samaria, and Jesus had to travel through it to go from Judah to Galilee. By the time Jesus reached the well, John tells us, in his frank avowal of Jesus' humanity, Jesus was tired (4.6). (For indications of Jesus' humanity, see also John 11.35 and 19.28.) Jesus remained at the well while his disciples went into the local town to buy food (4.8). And while Jesus rested there on his own, a woman made her way out to the well from the town where his disciples had gone, and was probably more than a little surprised when this lone man, quite obviously a Jew and a visitor to the area, addressed her. It was the first of many surprises in this conversation.

Jesus said to her, 'Will you give me a drink?' (4.7) It was a perfectly natural request given his tiredness and her means of drawing water from the well – she had a bucket to attach to the well's rope – along with her proficiency at a task she probably performed every day. But natural as the request was, it broke many established boundaries or barriers. It was not the usual etiquette, and perhaps she wondered what kind of a man he was and even whether it was just water that he wanted! In addressing this Samaritan woman, Jesus went against normal dealings between Jews and Samaritans, and between Jewish men and women. Jeremias, in his *Jerusalem in the time of Jesus,* writes: 'Eastern women took no part in public life. This was true of Judaism in the time of Jesus, in all cases where Jewish families faithfully observed the Law. When the Jewess of Jerusalem left her house, her face was hidden by an arrangement of two head veils, a headband on the forehead with bands to the chin, and a hairnet with ribbons and knots, so that her features could not be recognised. ... Any woman who went out without the headdress could be divorced. Accordingly a woman was to be unobserved in public' (Jeremias, pp. 359-360). But Jesus talked to this woman. Indeed he asked her for something, thereby putting himself in her debt.

Not only did Jesus cross the gender barrier but, more surprisingly, he crossed the Jewish/Samaritan barrier as well.

Samaria had been the capital of the Northern Kingdom of Israel after the division of the country following Solomon's reign (see 1 Kings 12), in fulfilment of the prophecy of 2 Samuel 12.10. Israel was occupied by Assyrian forces in the 7th century BC and subsequently re-settled by immigrants from within the Assyrian Empire. The Assyrians, as part of their policy of conquest, exiled part of the population of Israel/Samaria and settled different ethnic groups there as well. 'People from Babylon, Cuthah, Avva, Hamath, and Sepharvaim' were settled in Samaria (2 Kings 17.24ff). From then on the population became ethnically mixed, no longer purely Jewish, and the worship also became corrupt. 'Each national group made its own gods in the several towns where they settled, and set them up in the shrines the people of Samaria had made at the high places' (2 Kings 17.29). Such syncretistic worship, mixing the traditions of Israel with the pagan practices surrounding the deities of these immigrants, corrupted the worship of Israel. The result was that the Jews from Judah and elsewhere would have nothing to do with the Samaritans. In the 4th Century BC, a temple was established on Mt Gerizim where the Samaritans worshipped, and although there was a degree of rapprochement during the reign of Herod the Great, who took a Samaritan wife, by AD 9, after a Samaritan desecration of the Temple in Jerusalem, relations were once again at an all time low. Thus the 'woman at the well' said memorably to Jesus, 'You are a Jew and I am a Samaritan woman. How can you ask me for a drink?' Here John adds the comment, 'For Jews do not associate with Samaritans' (4.9). A Jew would certainly not drink out of the same bucket or water-jar as a Samaritan – such a thing would be deemed unthinkable and ceremonially unclean!

The conversation, while not leaving the metaphor of water, then acquires a different and more profound significance. The next few exchanges between Jesus and the woman play on the theme of water, provocatively, tantalisingly and intriguingly. While Jesus speaks of the living water that he can offer to satisfy spiritual thirst, a theme to which he returns in John 7.37-9, the woman understandably thinks more literally of the water in the well beside them. So they talk at cross-purposes for a little while. She takes his offer of 'living water' to mean a plentiful supply of water delivered without the arduous chore of going to the well each day to collect and carry the water for her household. Jesus raises the stakes in describing this living water as follows: 'Everyone who drinks this water will be thirsty again, but whoever drinks the water I give him will never thirst. Indeed, the water I give him will become in him a spring of water welling up to eternal life' (4.13-14). Here Jesus' water-talk passes well beyond her wildest imaginings and breaks any literal mould in which she has tried to contain his words and promise. She can only say 'Sir, give me this water so that I won't get thirsty and have to keep coming here to draw water' (4.15). Until this point the conversation seems to be a combination of verbal sparring and repartee, which threatens to miss its purpose: the woman thinks literally and Jesus speaks of something she cannot understand. And then he gently introduces into the conversation something that is real, heart stopping and uncanny, unless you know the power by which Jesus operates. It is also faintly unnerving.

What begins as unnerving becomes an unmasking. It starts with Jesus saying, 'Go, call your husband and come back' (4.16). Her denial that she has a husband is a half-truth; she already feels herself to be on shaky ground. And then full exposure follows, 'You are right when you say you have no husband. The fact is, you have had five husbands and the man you now have is not your husband. What you have just said is quite true' (4.17-18).

Suddenly the conversation has moved to a different level. What began as banter about water on her part has suddenly exposed the sadness and perhaps sordidness of her life. She can put on an air of bravado and wit, but it masks a deeper sadness of broken relationships and some degree of isolation. Jesus treats her honestly, but gently. He puts the best gloss on her answer 'I have no husband.' He says firstly, 'You are right when you say you have no husband...you have had five,' and again at the end he says, 'What you have just said is quite true'. Yes, she may be technically correct, but she knows very well it hardly describes the reality of her life. But she is not done yet. She is used to living off her wits, and she deflects the conversation whilst acknowledging his insight. 'Sir, I can see you are a prophet.' She acknowledges the truth of what he has just said whilst leaving its significance unremarked.

Then she subtly turns the conversation away from this uncomfortable moment. She brings up the vexed question of the Jewish-Samaritan divide: 'Our fathers worshipped on this mountain (Mt Gerizim) but you Jews claim that the place where we must worship is in Jerusalem' (4.20). How genuinely interested the Samaritan woman was in this question we cannot be sure, but Jesus gives her a remarkable reply. He does not avoid her question and say, 'Let's get back to your life'; rather, he answers her question fully, prophetically and powerfully. He talks about worshipping the Father; he affirms the primacy of the Jews in God's plan of salvation, but he also speaks of the coming of a new age in which worship will be conducted differently.

At the heart of Jesus' reply is that worship will not be place-specific, that is, related to particular holy places. Indeed, you could rightly argue that it was never intrinsically related to place in the first instance, be it Jerusalem, Gerizim, Bethel or Shiloh, or any of the Old Testaments sites traditionally related to worship. The exiles learnt that although far from Jerusalem in Babylon – by whose waters they sat down and wept and where they were unable to sing the Lord's song in a strange land (see Psalm 137), God could still be worshipped, even as the life of Daniel made clear (Daniel 6.10). The Psalmist tells us that we are unable to flee from his presence (see Psalm 139.7ff), and so we may be conscious of his presence with us anywhere. Indeed David was told, when proposing the temple as a future place of Jewish worship, that God could not be contained in one place, though graciously he would be worshipped and known in the Temple when built (see 1 Chronicles 17.4ff). But now Jesus says to the Samaritan woman the time for such locations for worship is drawing to a close. God will be worshipped anywhere, wherever and whenever his Spirit moves people in worship: '(for) a time is coming and has now come when the true worshippers will worship the Father in spirit and truth, for they are the kind of worshippers the Father seeks' (4.23). It is easy to underestimate the importance of this saying that true worship is now worldwide, wherever the Spirit and truth inspires a person. But what is more extraordinary is that that this movement of worship from Jerusalem to the ends of the earth is announced to a sinful Samaritan woman who Jesus met one midday when he was tired and she came out to draw water.

This talk of future worship rings a deep theological bell in the woman and she quite rightly associates this new age of worship with the coming of the Messiah. So she says, 'I know that Messiah' (called the Christ) is coming. When he comes he will explain everything' (4.25). What delicious irony, since that is exactly what Jesus has already been doing: 'explaining everything'. And what better cue in this conversation for Jesus to say, 'I who speak to you am he' (4.26).

The results of this conversation were numerous. The disciples were surprised to see Jesus talking to this Samaritan woman, but dared not ask why he was talking to her – she being a Samaritan and a woman (4.27). The woman herself gave testimony about Jesus, asking whether he was the Christ (4.29). Jesus talked to his disciples about another form of food, which he called 'doing and finishing the Father's will' (see 4.34). And lastly, the woman's testimony about Jesus was that 'he told me everything I ever did.' (Maybe her statement was a little embellished or exaggerated, but it must have *seemed* that way to her!). It brought her fellow townsfolk out to meet Jesus, who then turned his visit to the well into a mini-mission to the town of Sychar. Many believed. A conversation with a single woman led to a crowd of believers!

Study Questions

What barriers did Jesus cross in speaking to this woman? What barriers are we called to cross today?

What is the benefit of explaining Christian truth in metaphors? Why did Jesus use a running metaphor here?
What was the turning point of the conversation and why?

What would give reality and spiritual conviction to our conversations with people about God?

How did Jesus deal with the 'religious' questions that the woman brought up? What kind of religious or moral questions are we likely to face today?

What is the significance of the new way of worship that Jesus speaks about here?

What was the woman's testimony which communicated with her own friends and why? What cuts ice today?

What does Jesus explain to the disciples about his *food?*

A 'chance' conversation by a well becomes a mission to a whole town with many believers resulting – what was at the heart of this mission?

What do you learn from this conversation, especially?

Study 5

A Conversation with a woman caught in the act

John 7.53-8.11

You may have noticed that most of the conversations we have looked at so far have illustrated themes that John first put forward in the prologue of the gospel. The conversation with Mary at the wedding in Cana illustrates Jesus' generosity: 'From the fullness of his grace we have all received one blessing after another' (1.16); after the Law brought by Moses, a new era of grace is beginning with Jesus (1.17). The conversation with Nicodemus illustrated the truth that 'to all who received him, to those who believed in his name, he gave the right to become children of God – children born not of natural descent, nor of human decision or a husband's will, but born of God' (1.12-13). The conversation with the woman at the well illustrated supremely that 'in him was life, and that life was the light of men' (1.4). In this story of the woman caught in adultery, in which she is dragged as a shameful exhibit into the power play between the teachers of the law, the scribes and Jesus, another great principle set out in the prologue is

35

displayed, which is that 'grace and truth came through Jesus Christ' (1.17).

Perhaps nowhere in the gospel is this combination of grace and truth in the words and actions of Jesus more vividly displayed than in this conversation with the woman caught in adultery and her accusers. The only other place where grace and truth is more wonderfully made known is in the crucifixion.

This combination of grace and truth is greatly needed in our broken and confused world, not least in the area of our sexuality. Truth can too easily become a harsh rendering of judgement on another; and compassion or grace can too easily slip into a *laissez-faire* (i.e. leave it alone) attitude that permits anything that is deemed loving. The conversation with the woman caught in adultery is instructive, since we see Jesus acting with both grace and mercy, but also with moral challenge.

In John's gospel truth is a primary value and it has the power to set you free, but it is wielded in grace.[4] Grace is God's undeserved favour that does not condemn us for our failings, but rather seeks a way forward through forgiveness and restoration. Few things are harder to achieve than this balance of grace and truth in life and ministry that Jesus achieved. His truth was never remote and simply judgemental; his grace never insipid and without moral content. Each characteristic was strong in itself, but also complementary to the other.

We note that although this story is not in any of the oldest complete manuscripts of the New Testament, like *Codex Vaticanus* and *Codex Sinaiticus*, it does occur in a much less well-attested manuscript simply called 'D'.[5] The story is referred to by Papias, an early church leader and Bishop of Hierapolis (60-130AD). It could well be a fragment from another gospel, which was then attached to John. Nonetheless, it is there in our Bible, with the explanation that its provenance or source is questionable. But the tenor of the story sounds so authentic, and

---

[4] See *Word from the Throne*, pp. 35ff
[5] Morris L., *The Gospel According to St John*, Eerdmans, 1971, p. 882

the action of Jesus so in keeping with his style and demeanour, that it has the ring of integrity and authenticity about it, and it is regarded as authentic even though it may not originally have been part of John's gospel. For these reasons it was no doubt included and placed here.

The story is well known. A group of scribes and Pharisees bring a woman who has been caught in the act of adultery to Jesus while he is teaching in the Temple courts. It seems she was either caught by some of them or by others who then handed her over to these scribes and Pharisees. At any rate, she was a pawn in their running conflict with Jesus, a tasteless exhibit in an essentially theological confrontation between Jesus and themselves, in which they sought to compromise him, discredit him and dent his popularity or reputation for orthodoxy, or all of these. It was, as we know, highly tendentious or unfair, since they brought only the woman – yet if caught in the act of adultery the man must have been present too! The man was left behind in a complete negation of the Law, for he was equally culpable under the terms of Deuteronomy 22.23-27. Despite their injustice in bringing *only* the woman, they sought a ruling from Jesus as to whether the Mosaic sentence should now be passed on her. It was of course a trap (8.6), so that they could bring a charge against him (Jesus) in the Jewish courts.

The trap was in essence not dissimilar to the one that was set over whether to pay taxes (see Mark 12.13ff) to Caesar. The question was: will Jesus violate Mosaic Law or Roman law in the judgment he gives? To permit the stoning would violate Roman law, which did not allow the death penalty to be inflicted without recourse to the magistrates, but not to do so would violate Mosaic Law, which called for such a punishment. Jesus knew what they were up to! Still seated, in the customary posture of a teaching Rabbi, he hardly looked at these hectoring and vociferous men who sought to condemn the woman. Instead he began with his finger to write in the dust.

At this point the conversation falls into two parts: one with the group of scribes and Pharisees and the other with the woman herself. Firstly Jesus turns his attention to the accusers who are bitterly calling on him to give his verdict. His body language is interesting. He hardly makes eye contact with them, bending over and writing in the dust with his finger. He then stands up and faces them, delivering his memorable judgement, and then he resumes his seated position and continues his doodling or writing in the dust. What is he writing and why? I have heard it suggested that he was writing the names of the Scribes' or Pharisees' mistresses in the sand to demonstrate their hypocrisy, but that is simply conjectural or even fanciful! I have heard that after the fashion of Roman judges he was writing his judgement in the dust, as Roman judges used to write down their judgement and sentence before delivering it. This may be closer to the mark, but why then resume his seated posture and continue writing (see 8.8)? It could simply be that he was vexed by their moral hypocrisy which he was soon to expose, and looked for something to do which displayed his impatience and anger with them and their treatment of this woman.

At any rate Jesus' answer to their question of whether Moses' law of stoning for adultery should be enforced was, 'If any one of you is without sin, let him be the first to throw a stone at her' (8.7). It was a brilliant and devastating challenge to their sense of moral superiority. It was not that Jesus said that only if a person had not committed adultery might he throw the first stone, but that anyone who was without *any* sin at all could throw the first stone. On such a basis no one could now stone another, for all are disqualified by sin. Jesus, it seems, reforms the Mosaic Law with this saying and ends its death penalty. Having issued his challenge Jesus resumes writing in the dust and leaves his words to take effect on the consciences of the woman's accusers. It is interesting to see that older scribes or Pharisees slink away first, their consciences being more realistic, and their spirit made a little humbler by age. The younger ones may have been more self-confident, more aggressive and assertive. But once the older ones leave, it is then more likely that no one will hurl the first stone, as it is now tantamount to a declaration of complete moral purity, which already a number of the more senior scribes or Pharisees in the group have disavowed by leaving. One by one they leave, no doubt deflated and somewhat chastened. Their religious game is up, it has rebounded on them! And then only the woman who has not yet spoken is left standing in front of Jesus and their brief conversation begins.

'Woman, where are they? Has no one condemned you?' Jesus asks. And then she speaks her only words in this conversation: 'No one, sir'. 'Then neither do I condemn you. Go now and leave your life of sin' (8.11). Here we see the combination of grace and truth at work; the fulfilment in action of what we read in the Prologue (1.14). Jesus neither condemns nor condones. He does not condemn, but nor does he leave her as she is; instead he challenges her to leave 'your life of sin.' To be on the side of truth is to face up to our responsibility, to live life with integrity, to maintain both loving and faithful relationships, to aim for the gold standard of human relationships both sexually and socially. To be on the side of grace is to forgive and move on, to overlook and not to rake over, to hope for the future rather than be bound by the past. By on the one hand telling her to leave her life of sin, Jesus did not compromise the Mosaic standard laid down in the Torah or Law, but, on the other, by telling her that he did not condemn her, he showed that he was for new beginnings rather than writing someone off as being unable to change and condemned already. The old way was sterile but the new way gave an opportunity for a fresh start.

This combination of grace and truth in dealing with moral, personal and sexual issues today could not be more important, especially as the church faces an increasingly diverse society. It is quite clear that society generally is word resistant, but it can still be reached and touched by compassionate action. It is interesting to see that Jesus paid careful attention to *what* he said as well as to *how* he said it, i.e. truth must be in the right *tone* to be heard (see the important verses on this in John 12.49-50). Too shrill and our words are not listened to; too *pianissimo* and they just become mood music, lost in the *muzak* of the age. (It is quite probable that the group will have several first hand experiences of these issues from close family or colleagues at work – pray for an honest and truly helpful discussion. What is the best way to approach these moral issues today?).

Study Questions

What was the intention of the scribes and Pharisees in bringing this unfortunate woman to Jesus?

What was the dilemma that they sought to place Jesus in, and what did they hope for?

Why was Jesus writing in the sand? What did his body language convey? What was brilliant about Jesus' reply to the scribes and Pharisees?

Why do you think it was the oldest Pharisees or scribes who slunk away first? (8.9)

In what way did Jesus' reply to the woman exemplify him being full of grace and truth?

What would this woman have needed following this trauma if she was to change?

How should we react to moral issues in our own day, especially those linked to personal relationships and sexuality?

What does a church 'full of grace and truth' look like? Do you belong to one, and how does it exemplify this?

Summarise.

Study 6

A Conversation with two sisters by a grave

John 11.1-57

The conversation at Lazarus' grave is one of the most extraordinary conversations in any of the gospels. Its context, emotion, promise and outcome make it exceptional. Wrapped as it is around probably greatest of the seven signs in the gospel of John, exhibiting as it does the reality of the great 'I am' saying – 'I am the resurrection and the life'– it has a focus and intensity which is common to perhaps only two other conversations: those with Pilate and Peter which we shall come to soon. It also proceeds from a close and deep relationship with the two sisters, and with Lazarus their brother.

Jesus, it seems, was a reasonably regular visitor to the home of Martha, Mary and Lazarus. There are accounts of him staying with them in at least one other gospel (Luke 10.38-42). In Luke we have the famous account of Jesus and his disciples visiting their home in Bethany, an occasion in which the characters of the two sisters are vividly revealed: Martha active, conscientious, prone to anxiety or *stress* as we would say today; Mary, by contrast, reflective, contemplative, thoughtful and seemingly unperturbed by the practical needs of the occasion (or if she was, happy to let them take their course.) Later she was to make a memorable and extravagant act of prophetic devotion to Jesus, wiping his feet with her hair and anointing him with very expensive and exotic perfume (John 11.1-11). And so it was that when Jesus stayed in their house that day, Mary sat at the Lord's feet soaking up all that the Lord was saying, while Martha busied herself in the kitchen bringing together a meal for at least 16 people, if all the disciples were there. Seeing Mary seated peacefully at the Lord's feet, she famously complained 'Lord, don't you care that my sister has left me to do all the work by myself? Tell her to help me!' (Luke 10.40). You can almost feel the frustration across the centuries. But Jesus equally famously replied, 'Martha, Martha' (using her name twice to reach the inner core of her being, and show affection at the same time), 'you are worried and upset about many things, but only one thing is needed. Mary has chosen what is better, and it will not be taken away from her' (10.41-42). Some of us may sympathise with Martha; after all, someone had to do the work, keep the show on the road, demonstrate hospitality. But then again Jesus was probably only there for a short time, therefore surely better to sit and listen to him.

'Only one thing is needed' is a compelling phrase – we do well to think about that in the strains and stresses of modern life where the pressures of image, results, success, work, money and relationships crowd in on us like wasps around a jar of jam on a summer's day. Yes, they can sting us too! But what is the one thing that is needful amidst all the demands clamouring for our attention? Sometimes we need to go away from our situation to accurately reflect on our lives and gain perspective. I am privileged to go to Africa to lead missions, and in a quiet moment in the morning or at sunset with the smoke of an African village wending its way to the sky or the dawn chorus of the birds welcoming in another day, it is possible to sieve through the many aspects of my life that clamour for attention and be left with the rock of *the one thing* that is really needful! As Alison Morgan writes, 'We live in a society which looks for gratification but craves belonging, looks for wealth and success but craves relationship ... a society which invests billions in developing drugs to combat the depression, anxiety and emptiness lurking within its members.'[6] What is the one thing that is needful? Simply to sit and listen to what Jesus has to say to us about our living. To sit and listen is not so easy in a society crowded with noise clamouring for our attention.

All this is preparation for the conversation that took place between Jesus and the sisters near the grave of their brother. But before we look at the conversation we must observe the context. Before he even arrived at Bethany, Jesus knew that Lazarus was gravely ill. A telling message had been sent to Jesus by the sisters: 'Lord, the one you love is sick' (John 11.3). It was like a message between close friends. The sisters knew that Jesus cared for, indeed loved, Lazarus. And John in an editorial remark says a little later, 'Jesus loved Martha and her sister and Lazarus' (11.5). Presumably the point here is that although Jesus in one sense loved all people, there are particular people who were especially close to him, of whom he was especially fond. Among these were the Apostle John, the beloved disciple, this family, the rich young ruler (see Mark 10.21; John 13.1) and his own mother (John 19.26). As a human he was drawn to particular people, as the Son of God he loved all. And yet despite the message of the sisters, despite the urgency of their request and the danger of his sickness, Jesus remained where he was and did not come immediately. Why was that? He said it was better for them that he remained where he was. In effect he allowed Lazarus to die so that he might raise him again to life. 'This sickness will not end in death. No, it is for God's glory so that God's Son may be glorified through it' (11.4).

---

[6] Alison Morgan, *The Wild Gospel,* Monarch 2004, p.305.

Jesus delayed and when he knew in his spirit that Lazarus had died, he returned to Judea, to Bethany, just a few miles from Jerusalem, back into the cauldron of confrontation between himself and the Jewish authorities. The disciples were well aware of the dangers. Some said, 'A short while ago the Jews tried to stone you' (presumably John 8.59). Thomas said in sheer bravado, 'Let us also go, that we might die with him' (11.16). So Jesus went to wake Lazarus from 'sleep', Jesus' favourite metaphor, it seems, for death; but the atmosphere he found in Bethany was one already deep in the throes of grief and mourning.

On arrival Jesus found that Lazarus had been dead for four days. The conversation was to be three ways: with Martha, with Mary and finally, in a sense, with their dead brother, Lazarus, who responded to the word of Christ. The first part of the conversation is covered in 11.17-27 and was with Martha. When Martha heard that Jesus was in the vicinity she went out to meet him. Ever the active, responsible and energetic elder sister, she went out to meet Jesus, grieving, but not paralysed or disabled by her grief. Her opening remark may have had a hint of reproach that Jesus had not arrived sooner, for she said, 'Lord, if you had been here, my brother would not have died.' If Jesus had come sooner when first called for by the sisters, he surely would have healed Lazarus. Even so Martha believed that 'even now God will give whatever you ask.' One wonders what she had in mind: resurrection now or at some point in the future? Jesus responded a little enigmatically, 'Your brother will rise again' (11.23), which Martha took to mean, in common with Jewish belief (except amongst the Sadducees – see Mark 12.18), that Lazarus would rise in the general resurrection. She said she believed that.

Jesus then said something extraordinary about himself in the '*I am*' saying with which the Anglican prayer book starts every funeral or thanksgiving service. The words are resonant with hope and meaning: 'I am the resurrection and the life. He who believes in me will live, even though he dies; and whoever lives and believes in me will never die. Do you believe this?' (11.25-26) It seems that Jesus was giving Martha sure grounds for hope and a firm challenge to belief or faith. Of course hope comes from faith; without faith there can be no hope of this kind. The hope is twofold: that the believing person will live even though he dies and the believing person will in a real sense never die. Yes, in one sense we must all pass through death, but death to Jesus is *sleep*: it does not extinguish our lives, which continue in a new form (like *angels,* see Mark 12.25), and in continuity with our former existence, (see 1 Corinthians 15.42ff). Having made this statement, Jesus threw out a challenge, 'Do you believe this?' (11.26). For in believing we have hope of things yet unseen.

One wonders whether this conversation with Martha was especially suited to her. It was strong, challenging and comforting at the same time. It demanded something from her: courage and faith and hope. And to Jesus' challenge, she was able to rise: 'Yes, Lord I believe that you are the Christ, the Son of God, who was to come into the world' (11.27). Even before the raising of her brother she did believe. Unlike her sister, she would not sit at the Lord's feet and extravagantly anoint him for burial with costly perfume, but her faith was nonetheless robust, her hope well founded. Her energy and active nature were channelled into this firm avowal of faith. For Martha comfort rested on this clear promise of Jesus, that in him were resurrection and life. There are many who approach grief in such a way: on the surface they do not appear emotional, nevertheless they seek the firm knowledge that in the end all will be well, and that resurrection will succeed death. This Jesus promised, and Martha believed him.

The meeting with Mary was rather different.

When her conversation with Jesus ended, Martha returned home and found Mary. Jesus remained outside the village, presumably unwilling to enter it because of not wishing to be caught up with the grief and mourning that was going on there. Martha took the message to Mary, 'The Teacher is here, and is asking for you' (11.28). There is little doubt that Jesus loved Mary, as well as the whole family. As soon as Mary heard that he was asking after her, she quickly left the house and went to him, followed by other mourning friends (11.29). Arriving where he was, Mary fell at his feet and said, like her sister, 'Lord, if you had been here, my brother would not have died'. Since they said the same thing to Jesus, these may have been words that they said to each other as they waited for the arrival of Jesus in the final stages of Lazarus' illness. If only he had come sooner and not been delayed then their brother would not have died.

If the meeting with Martha had been one of plain speaking, even challenging, with little evident grief being shown, the meeting with Mary and those who followed her could not have been more different. In place of a challenge to faith came the comfort of acute empathy; in place of the assertion of extraordinary power and authority in the 'I am' saying of Jesus to Martha, came the most expressive moment of solidarity with the fragility of human life in the face of death. Jesus, seeing the emotion of Mary and those who followed her, did not speak of what he *would* do or *could* do, he simply wept. '"Where have you laid him?" he asked. "Come and see, Lord," they replied. Jesus wept. Then the Jews said, "See how he loved him!"'(11.34-36). There is no doubt that Jesus, like John, who himself must have seen this event for himself and who alone records this miracle, was 'deeply moved in spirit and troubled' (11.33).

Although they began similarly, the two meetings with the two sisters could not have been more different: one appealing to faith and creating hope, the other through solidarity of emotion leading to action. The tears that Jesus shed and the feelings that he had, led him to action and to perform the miracle that all along he knew he would do (11.4). Going to the grave with the sisters, he asked for the removal of the stone. Ever the practical one, Martha pointed out that by this time there would be a bad smell; after all it was now four days since Lazarus died. Yet with the Apostle John, symbolism is never far away from the words and actions he records. The removal of the stone, allowing a bad odour to spread, could also be like the action of lifting the lid on the stone of grief. Underneath this stone of grief there can be a host of other feelings like resentment about being left, self-pity, anger, confusion or guilt. Loss of a loved one can be mixed with any of these feelings too. But Jesus gently rebuked her, 'Did I not tell you that if you believed, you would see the glory of God?' (11.40)

46

He prayed when the stone was taken away. He was assured that his Father had already heard him. His conversation, if that is what we can call it, with a dead man, was brief: 'Lazarus, come out!'

So extraordinarily dramatic was this event of a man coming out of a tomb wrapped in grave clothes, his hands and feet wrapped in strips of linen, that artists have paid much attention to it. It was a glorious and unmistakeable demonstration of God's glory and power; it was a sign of the divinity of Jesus and it was the consequence of love and compassion towards this family. This miracle was also a catalyst. Some Jews believed, others were hardened in their hearts and began conspiring against Jesus, fearing that his very success would jeopardise both the nation and the Temple (11.48). The Sanhedrin was called. The High Priest prophesied unwittingly that one man would die for the nation (11.50). Jesus withdrew with his disciples to the edge of the desert, to a village called Ephraim (11.54). There he waited for Passover. Six days before Passover Jesus re-emerged into public view once more at Bethany where Mary anointed him (John 12.1-11). It was only a week before he would be crucified, laid in a tomb and then the Father, by the Spirit, would raise *him* from the dead.

Study Questions

Why did Jesus delay in going to Bethany?

Why is sleep (v11-13) a good metaphor for death, what does it convey?

In what ways are Martha and Mary different in character? What is good about both of them?

In what ways were the conversations between Jesus and Martha and Mary different? Can you account for the difference?

What have you found helpful in meeting and talking to people in the early stages of grief?

Why are some people frightened or embarrassed by grief?

Why did Jesus weep?

What might 'taking off the grave clothes' be a metaphor for? (see 11. 44)

What effect did this miracle have in the Jewish community (see 11.45ff, 12.17-19).

What does this miracle tell us about hope?

Study 7

A Conversation with his Father

John 17.1-26

In our last study, we left Jesus having raised Lazarus from the dead and in conversation with Martha and Martha. Since then, in the narrative of John's gospel and as anticipated by Jesus (see 11.8ff), the temperature of confrontation between him and the Jewish authorities has been significantly raised. The conspiracy to end Jesus' life is now openly advanced by discussion in the Sanhedrin, the Jewish ruling council, which is called expressly for the purpose of dealing with Jesus (11.47,53). Caiaphas, the High Priest that year, 'prophesies' without being aware of it that 'it would be better for you (the Sanhedrin) that one man (should) die for the people than the whole people perish' (11.50). Jesus withdraws temporarily from the spotlight and remains in a deserted place called Ephraim.

Eventually, six days before the Passover, Jesus moves closer to Jerusalem to Bethany where he is anointed by Mary (12.3). And characteristically, at this dinner given in honour of Jesus, Martha *serves* (12.2). Jesus then enters Jerusalem triumphantly, openly provoking the authorities by coming to the city as their King, meekly riding on a donkey. Jesus is now entirely focussed on his upcoming passion, with no time for interviews with enquiring Greeks who come to speak with him (12.20-21), saying instead 'The hour has come for the Son of Man to be glorified' (12.23). Jesus proclaims that when he is lifted up on the Cross, he will draw all men to himself (12.32).

He celebrates the Last Supper with his disciples just before the Passover feast (13.1-2), and washes their feet. And 'having loved his own who were in the world, he now showed them the full extent of his love' not only by washing their feet but by dying for them and 'for all the scattered children of God, to bring them together and make them one' (11.52).

The washing of the disciples' feet is followed by Jesus' longest discourse or conversation with them, known as the Upper Room Discourse. It begins in the Upper Room and then moves outside to the Temple courts (15.1). The context is the imminent departure and passion of Jesus. His teaching centres on that event, as well as on the work of the Holy Spirit after his departure, the onset of persecution of the church, and yet the gifts of joy and peace that will then be theirs. At the end of this discourse Jesus prays, probably in the Temple area, before he leaves for Gethsemane and the final hours before his arrest. In that context and at that juncture Jesus prays his longest recorded prayer to his Father, which is sometimes called his Highly Priestly prayer. It is a solemn conversation with his Father, which concludes his earthly ministry before the events of the passion and the first Easter day.

The prayer or conversation is notable for its insight into Jesus' relationship with his Father. More than any other gospel writer, John shows us the inner working of that relationship with the Father. In the synoptic gospels (Matthew, Mark and Luke, which derive their name *synoptic* from their sharing of common material), there are only brief glimpses of that relationship between the Father and the Son, principally at Jesus' Baptism and Transfiguration. On those occasions the Father says of the Son, 'This is my Son, whom I love; with him I am well pleased' (Matthew 3.17; see also Mark 1.11 and Luke 3.22). And on the occasion of his Transfiguration, Luke records the Father saying, 'This is my Son, whom I have chosen: listen to him.' (Luke 9.35; see also Matthew 17.5 and Mark 9.7. Interestingly, John does not record the Transfiguration in his gospel.) But whereas these are the principal interactions between Father and Son in the synoptic gospels, in John that relationship is much more deeply revealed.

In John's gospel, the qualities of that relationship are consistently revealed throughout as being complete dependence, trust, mutual love and acknowledgement of one another's true being and status in the Godhead. This element of dependence is shown through Jesus' avowed dependence on the Father for both his *words* and *works*. Words and works are, after all, the principal means whereby the wisdom and power of God are manifest in Jesus' life, and which together proclaim that he is the Word made flesh, has come from the Father and is returning to the Father (see 3.13). Jesus' words come from the Father (14.10); indeed as he says, the Father tells him not only *what* to say but *how* to say it (12.49). Likewise, the *works* that Jesus performed are given him by the Father. In both these ways Jesus shows complete dependence upon and trust in the Father, so it is not surprising that when Philip says 'Show us the Father', Jesus replies 'Don't you know me, Philip.... Don't you believe that I am in the Father, and that the Father is in me?' (14.8-10). Such is the complete identity between Father and Son. His teaching centres on his forthcoming passion, on the gift of the Spirit, on the onset of persecution and the gifts of joy and peace which will be theirs.

Jesus here demonstrates that dependence on the Father is of the essence of his ministry. His passion, that is, his offering of himself for the world, supremely in his crucifixion, will accomplish what he has come to do; but in so doing he will place himself entirely in the Father's hands. At this point he therefore says, 'Father, the time has come' (17.1), the moment towards which his whole life has been moving. The *time* that was not yet ripe at the wedding at Cana of

Galilee (2.4), nor after the raising of Lazarus (11.54ff), has now fully come. Now the Son of Man will be lifted up (3.14; 8.28 and 12.32ff) and he will be glorified and he will be able draw all people to himself.

Jesus opens his prayer with a request that the Father will now glorify his son. There is a hidden meaning here which we must explore. We are so used to a celebrity culture, that 'glory' tends to conjure ideas of someone looking svelte, well groomed, sleek, fashionable and surrounded by adoring hangers-on. But not so with Jesus. His glory was to be shown in a lonely deserted figure, abandoned by human justice and in the company of thieves, a few vulnerable women, including his mother, and a group of strangers alternately mocking or silently impressed, as in the case with his Roman executioners, the centurion and the guard. Glory would be in the inner revelation of his character of holy love and compassionate kingship to a discerning and watching world.[7] Glory would be shown in doing what no other person could do, which was atoning for the sins of the guilty and creating a way back to God. Jesus, as he himself recognised, had been given authority (17.2) to give eternal life to all those given to him by the Father. (Note again the complete integration or mutuality of Father and Son.) This gift of eternal life consists in a relationship (*knowing* being an important word to John: see also his Epistles) with both the Father and the Son. Jesus prays that just as he brought glory to the Father on earth by completing all that he has been given to do (speaking those words and fulfilling those actions), he will now be glorified in the greatest of all his works, the work of the cross and the most revealing of all his words, those spoken from the throne of Calvary. To glorify him will mean revealing the true and inner character of God in these words and actions.

Having prayed that he might be glorified in this way, Jesus prays for those whom the Father has given him, the disciples he formed as well as all future believers. There is a real sense in this prayer of Jesus having revealed to the disciples his relationship with the Father: he has revealed the Father's name or character to the disciples who were given to him (17.6); he has helped them to understand that he was

---

[7] See also Patrick Whitworth, *The Word from the Throne*, Ch. 6.

sent by the Father (17.8); they now understand the complete interdependence of Father and Son (17.7) and they will learn the truth of what Jesus says about his relationship with the Father, i.e., that 'all I have is yours, and all you have is mine' (17.10). In other words, the disciples have at the heart of their understanding, he says, the reality of this relationship between Father and Son. Now, nearly at the end of his earthly ministry and shortly before his return to his Father (see 17.11-13), Jesus is accounting for the disciples and their understanding and perspective. In some ways it is all the more amazing that Jesus makes the reality and genuineness of their discipleship so central both to his purpose in coming and so core to the future of his plans for the world.

What does Jesus pray for these disciples? There appear to be *four* things he prays for the disciples positively, and one thing he does not pray for!

Firstly he prays for their *protection*. Like a parent leaving children at school for the first time, Jesus is concerned for their protection or spiritual security, but he is *not* ultimately concerned for their physical safety. After all, he knows the dangers they be will be exposed to by virtue of following him, he knows that the world will hate them (17.14). But although they may not be physically safe always, he prays for their protection – meaning their spiritual well being – that they may be protected from the evil one (17.15). The protection we need is likewise from the evil one, from the dominating cares and anxieties of life, from trials that can potentially overwhelm us. How can we help each other in facing these?

Secondly he prays for *the transforming effect of his words*. There is no doubt Jesus' *words* are central to the forming of the disciples. Jesus has deliberately passed them on to the disciples in his teaching. He says, 'I gave them the words you gave me and they accepted them' (17.8). These words, slowly working from the inside out, fashioned them. No doubt with a many a misunderstanding, with many a slip up, with many further explanations of what he meant. But slowly and imperceptibly the word like seed in them grew and bore fruit. The word from the Word was delivered, and this would sanctify them for the task: 'Sanctify them by the truth: your word is truth' (17.17). Sanctify means make holy, but it also means being set apart for and made ready for the task.

Thirdly Jesus prays for their *mission*. Mission means to be sent, from the Latin word *missio* – to send. Jesus was sent by his Father, and he voluntarily embraced this mission. And now the disciples are sent into the world, to be the salt and light of the Kingdom. They are equipped by the Spirit, just as Jesus himself was equipped by the Spirit at the outset (see 1.32-33; 7.39; 20.22).They are to go as harbingers and models of the kingdom, infected with the selfsame joy that Jesus had (see 17.13). Likewise we are sent by Jesus into our streets, power structures, communities, schools, and places of work, to live as disciples: people of grace and truth, joy and compassion.

And *fourthly* Jesus prays for their unity (17.11). It is a request, which is further extended and emphasised in the last section of this prayer. The clue to this unity in what Jesus prays is that it is a *consequence* of being kept and protected by the power of the Father's name. Presumably his *name* means the character of God: his generosity, compassion, love, sense of justice and faithfulness. If we remain in him as described by these qualities, then we are more likely to keep the unity we have been given. And to be kept in that name is to live in the light of the character of God and in concert with it. But move outside of that *name* – those characteristics – and it will be hard to bring about that unity. Surely this has been borne out by experience. The disunity of the church down the ages has been due in large measure to the power of the sword (the state) being used to ensure the orthodoxy of the church. Rather, we are to keep the unity of the spirit through the bond of peace, as Paul says (Ephesians 4.3). And unity will become an important ingredient in mission. Where Christians are disunited, they are hardly credible; but where there is unity, there the Lord commands the blessing and what they say is far more convincing (Psalm 133).

Having prayed for his own disciples, Jesus now looks further into the future and prays for the future church, that is, for those who will believe by virtue of his own disciples' lives and witness. Furthermore, he prays in turn for those who will believe because of each successive generation of Christian witness. The prayer for unity in this section becomes even more imperative. Jesus prays, 'May they be brought to *complete unity* to let the world know that you sent me and have loved them even as you have loved me' (17.23). The quality of that unity will be similar to the unity between Father and Son (may they be one 'just as you are in me and I am in you' 17.21), which is an extraordinary prospect. Once again the sharing of God's glory, that is his shining character, is the means whereby that unity is brought about (17.22-24).

Looking back on Jesus' prayer we must say that very often the church has largely frustrated his desire and intercession. However, when such unity has been achieved through times of shared worship and mission, then undoubtedly there has been and still is much power and blessing.

Finally, one thing is clear: Jesus prays for the church, that is for his followers, rather than for the world in general (17.9). He specifically tells us he is not praying for the world. Rather he prays for the church *in* the world. His strategy for mission therefore appears to be that the church will change the world. The church, however weak and failing it may seem, is still to be the transforming agent in the world at large. The church is to be *in* the world but not *of* it (17.14); in the world but not succumbing to the evil one (17.15). In so far as the church has failed to live up to its calling there is deep reason for repentance, grief and renewed effort to be holy. In so far as it has failed to unite, there is also deep reason for repentance and new ways of recognising the gift of unity we have been given. In so far as we, the church, have been fractious and judgmental, then there is a renewed need for the church truly to know God's character or name and share in his glory (17.11,22).

I write this as further revelations about the church and its leaders have come to light. It does not matter whether they are in our bit of the church or not. It is a time for repentance, due shame and the good ordering of the church for the future. Our hope must be that the prayer of Jesus will yet be answered.

Study Questions

How do you see this prayer in the context of Jesus' ministry?

What does this prayer show us about Jesus' relationship with the Father?

What does Jesus pray for his disciples?

Why doesn't Jesus pray for the *world*? (In John's writing the world in this sense means society which does not acknowledge God).

How do you understand the word *glory* in this passage? In what ways is this different from celebrity culture?

What kind of unity can we work towards as Christians? How are we doing that as a church?

What kind of things damage or enhance unity?

How do you understand mission?

What does it mean to be in the world but not of it?

What note in general does the church especially need to strike at the moment in society at large?

If you wanted your church leader to say one thing to society today, what would it be and why?

Study 8

A Conversation with the Roman Governor

John 19.28-19.16

There are few, if any, more extraordinary conversations than the one between the Roman Governor, Pilate, and Jesus. Jesus is brought to Pilate from the house of Caiaphas, the High Priest, where he has been held and tried overnight. The trial has been a mockery of justice. The other gospel writers record in more detail the course of this trial before the High Priest. Matthew gives the fullest account. It was held before the Sanhedrin, the High Priest and the elders of the people. We are told that they 'were looking for false evidence to put against Jesus', but found none until two came forward saying that he had said: 'I am able to destroy the temple of God and rebuild it in the three days' (Matthew 26.61). Asked directly whether he was the Son of God, Jesus answered plainly 'Yes, it is as you say,' adding that 'in the future you will see the Son of Man sitting at the right hand of the Mighty One and coming on the clouds of heaven' (Matthew 2.64). This was enough for the High Priest, who tore his clothes declaring that Jesus had spoken blasphemy. The court agreed that he was worthy of death.

Meanwhile, outside the High Priest's house where this overnight trial had been hastily staged, standing in the courtyard was Peter. He had gained admittance, it seems, through the good offices of John, who apparently knew the High Priest's family (18.15-16). Previously so sure of himself and his loyalty to Jesus, but unprepared for the sudden turn of events of Jesus' arrest and trial, Peter denied knowing Jesus three times. It seems that around about the same time as the culmination of this trial and its verdict of blasphemy, the cock crowed and Jesus turned and looked at Peter (Luke 22.61). As Peter went outside the courtyard to weep, realising the full impact of his denial and the fulfilment of Jesus' earlier prediction that he would deny him three times before the cock crowed, the court decided to hand Jesus over to Pilate and request his death (18.28ff). By now it was early morning and the extraordinary conversation between prisoner and governor was about to begin.

Jerusalem was a close knit city numbering about 30,000 people of whom a large part were priests, Levites, Pharisees and Scribes. However, at Festival time the population doubled, with pilgrims arriving from throughout the Roman world. It was now Passover, and the city would have been teeming with people and the population would be at least 100,000. A triumvirate of power existed in Palestine/Judea: firstly, the Sanhedrin who had tried Jesus speciously overnight; secondly, one of the sons of Herod the Great, Herod the Tetrarch of Galilee (whose jurisdiction was confined to Galilee; see Luke 23.7), and thirdly, Pontius Pilate, representing Imperial Rome and appointed by Tiberius Caesar. Between them they exercised power over different aspects of Jewish life, but final authority rested with the Prefect Pilate and the garrison or legions, which were under his command. At least two legions would have been garrisoned in Judea and the sight of Roman soldiers and Roman power would have been familiar to all.

Having been tried by the High Priest and the Sanhedrin, or at least those who could be there (was Nicodemus present, I wonder?), Jesus was transferred to Pilate, since he alone could sentence the prisoner to death. Jesus appeared before Pilate already weary from a long night without sleep, as well as answering the taunts, slurs and false charges of the Jewish court. For John this trial by Pilate formed the centre of the judicial process, which brought about Jesus' eventual crucifixion. Indeed many of the themes, already present in the gospel, seem to be woven into this conversation.

At first Pilate wanted to know why the Sanhedrin or religious court, as Pilate would have understood it, wanted his involvement. Pilate was reluctant from the start. He smelt danger. His wife had already had premonitions of trouble, having dreamed about Jesus overnight. Her advice to Pilate as the trial got underway was 'Don't have anything to do with that innocent man, for I have suffered a great deal today in a dream because of him' (Matthew 27.19). The Jewish leaders were especially fastidious at this Passover time and were unwilling to enter the palace of such a notorious gentile as Pilate, and so forced him to come outside to meet them and the prisoner, Jesus, whom they brought with them. 'So Pilate went out to them' hearing of their approach and asked them, as any Roman would, 'what charges are you bringing against this man?' (John 18.29) They evaded the specific question, simply saying generally that he was a criminal and that he was worthy of death. To get this sentence, they had brought Jesus to Pilate. Pilate left the courtyard or balcony where he had met the Jewish leaders and returned inside the Palace to interrogate Jesus. He must have heard of him, even if he had never seen him before. Now Jesus was standing before him, defenceless, silent and completely in Pilate's hands. It must have been an extraordinary moment, full of tension and foreboding. Their conversation would revolve around the themes of kingship, power and truth, and would be constantly interrupted by Pilate's attempt to release him, or at the very least evade imposing the death penalty on one whom he knew to be innocent.

Going inside the palace Pilate straightaway said, 'Are you the king of the Jews?' (18.33) It was an interesting opener and in many ways went straight to the heart of the issue. How did Pilate know that Jesus had either implicitly or directly made such a claim? Yes, the crowd had at one point in Galilee tried to make Jesus a king (see John 6.15), but he had evaded their intention. Only a few days before, the whole city had been stirred by the arrival of Jesus seated on a donkey, riding into Jerusalem to the acclamation of the crowds (12.12ff). Knowing the religious leaders well and having offended their religious sensibilities on more than one occasion previously, Pilate could easily guess at the jealousy against Jesus and the desire to have him out of the way (see especially the reactions of the Pharisees, 12.19). Of course Pilate knew that if Jesus claimed *kingship* he would be making himself a rival to Caesar, as the Jewish leaders would be quick to point out later, but Pilate was intrigued to learn what kind of king Jesus purported to be. As so often, Jesus answered the question with a question of his own: 'Is that your own idea, or did others talk to you about me?' (18.34). After some bluster about the nature of the case and exasperation with the Jewish leaders, Pilate received what must have been an enigmatic answer: 'My kingdom is not of this world. If it were, my servants would fight to prevent my arrest by the Jews. But now my kingdom is from another place' (18.36). A kingdom for which its members did not fight, which came from another place – whatever that might be! Pilate concluded that amongst it all Jesus was a king: 'You are a king, then!' (18.37). Jesus concurred, 'You are right in saying I am a king. In fact, for this reason I was born, and for this I came into the world, to testify to truth. Everyone on the side of truth listens to me' (18.37). Nowhere was Jesus more explicit about his kingship than here, when the representative of the greatest imperial power on earth confronted him. Conscious of the fading of the empires of the world, Jesus was only too aware of the eternal nature of his kingdom. It is a kingdom about which he had been teaching for three years, especially in his parables and which, by his death and resurrection, he was about to inaugurate.

But just as it seemed that the question of kingship was answered and Jesus had said that that he was a king, albeit of a different kind from the world's idea of kingship, Jesus introduced a new concept to the conversation: truth. 'Everyone,' he said, 'on the side of truth listens to me.' Not surprisingly Pilate asked, 'What is truth?' (12.38) This time Pilate did not wait for the reply, but went outside to tell the Jews that he had found no basis for a charge against him and suggested that he release Jesus, 'the King of the Jews,' to them in accordance with the custom of releasing a prisoner to them at Passover (12.39). They cried for Barabbas instead. But Pilate's question was a central one: What is truth? The whole gospel was about truth. It is an important word for Jesus and also for John in the communication of Jesus' message and the construction of the gospel. At the outset we are told that Jesus came as the Word made flesh full of grace and truth (1.14). The truth of who he was, his identity, was central to the debate between Jesus and the Jews (see 5.31-47; 7.18; 14.6). We are to worship in Spirit and in truth (4.23) and if we know the truth, the truth will set us free. Jesus is the very embodiment of truth: truth about God and who he is; truth about humans and what purpose they have and how they can be free to pursue that purpose (2.25), and truth about the future and what will endure to the end. In other words, the kingship of Jesus will endure eternally because it rests on truth and in knowing the truth about God and ourselves we unlock the way to fulfilment. All else is sinking sand and all kingdoms based on anything other than the truth will in the end crumble. That has been the message of history. Empires come and go, including the one whose representative was Jesus' judge in Jerusalem that day. Only the empire which is based on reality will survive, for that is based on truth. In the days of the Soviet Union, the main and only newspaper was *Pravda*, the state controlled newspaper. Its name meant truth but it printed mostly propaganda for the state, a lot of which was based on falsehood. It was no surprise that in the end the empire of which *Pravda* was an integral part collapsed, unable to mask the truth that was staring all in the face, namely economic paralysis, internal corruption in the Communist party and military collapse. The lie could not run forever; the truth had to be known.

When Pilate went outside to confront the Jewish leaders once more, his options for freeing Jesus were running out. He had said there was no evidence for a charge against him (19.4). He tried a prisoner exchange, but they cried for Barabbas. He had sent Jesus to Herod the Tetrarch as he heard that Jesus was a Galilean, but Herod had sent him back (Luke 23.11). Lastly Pilate had sought to satisfy the blood lust of the Jews by having Jesus flogged: a brutal punishment that often killed the prisoner because of its appalling severity. But even this did not appease their desire for Jesus' execution. They still, cried 'Crucify him, Crucify him'. In this bleeding and tortured state, dressed in a purple robe – a sign of nobility and kingship, albeit ironically bestowed, since the soldiers were mocking Jesus' claim – and a crown of thorns pressed on his head, Pilate embarked on the final part of the conversation. It was about power.

Jesus remained silent (see also 1 Peter 2.23). Pilate thought himself between a rock and a hard place: between a prisoner who, it seemed, refused to defend himself, and a mob of religious leaders unjustly bent on Jesus' blood. So Pilate went inside the Governor's Palace once again and said to Jesus, 'Don't you realise I have power either to free you or to crucify you?' Jesus responded, 'You would have no power over me if it were not given to you from above' (19.11). One man, Pilate, thought he had the power to grant freedom or death, while the other man, Jesus, seemingly having *no* power, said to the person who seemingly had power that he only had power because it was granted to him from *above*. The prisoner said in effect he and his Father are the source of all power, and the man who thought he had power finds that it is held on trust and will be accountable for its use. In the narrative of Jesus' trial, we find *three* power centres at work: the Jews who hand Jesus over to Pilate, whom Jesus says have the greater responsibility for manipulating power and using it to their own jealous ends (v11); Pilate who has been given power to administer justice and likewise holds that exercise of power on trust; and *thirdly* the prisoner who looks *powerless* and *defenceless* but is the source of all authority and power. For he is the Word made flesh '(through) whom all things were made: (and) without him nothing was made that has been made' (1.3). All power is held on trust and those who exercise it will be accountable for their use of it.

Pilate knew how he should act. He knew that the prisoner was innocent. He knew that the Jewish leaders wanted a judicial murder to rid them of the challenge Jesus brought. He knew that there was no proper evidence for a charge of sedition against Jesus. His kingdom was not political or military; it was a kingdom of another world or at least another order. It posed a threat to all empires, but there was no credible evidence against it, except healing the sick, opening the eyes of the blind, making the lame walk and the deaf hear. But Pilate would not do what he should do. The crowd and their crying for Jesus' blood intimidated him. And the threat that some might report him as not being a friend of Caesar was perhaps the nail in the coffin of his principled objection to executing Jesus. Until then he had sought to set Jesus free, but his will to carry through his nobler convictions caved in. He famously washed his hands (not included in John's account), but responsibility was not so easily discharged. It was more abdication than resolution. Jesus was handed over for execution, as he knew he would be, but not before one more prophetic irony.

Earlier Pilate had brought Jesus out to the crowd after his flogging and with evident relish said, 'Here is the man' or 'Behold the Man' (19.5) – *Ecce Homo*. For Pilate it was surely a way of saying to the crowd 'what are you concerned about, he is like any other man: here he stands before you bloodied by Roman punishment. Here he is, mocked and flogged; what now of his revolution of love and his hope of a new Kingdom? He is just like any other man.' But he wasn't, and he isn't! In fact he is the man: the paradigm man, the second Adam, the pattern for all human living. There is no one else like him.

And then, as if to add one final prophetic irony to the mix, Pilate brought Jesus out one last time and said, 'Here is your King' (19.14). Again, he might have been saying, 'So what are you frightened of? Look at him: your king.' But in a sense he was never more king than in that moment. Suffering, weak, defenceless, on the way to the cross in a matter of minutes, yes, but nevertheless exhibiting all the marks of kingship, which would triumph in his kingdom and mark it out as different from all other empires. He was the king and he would in time be glorified as such in an unmistakeable way. So Jesus was the example for humans: he was *the* man, *the* human. He was the example of all kingship, he was *the* king, the ruler for all to emulate, *the* one who rightly administered power. And ironically Pilate declared him as such in what was a piece of ironic admiration for a man whom at the very least he admired, but could not set free.

Study Questions

Why do you think John gives so much space to this conversation?

What lies at the heart of this conversation?

How doers Jesus conduct himself in this conversation?

What does it teach us about the handling of power?

Where do you exercise power and authority? What principles guide you in the exercise of authority both in the church and the world?

Why is power so often mismanaged in the world or church?

What memorable phrases or actions are there in this conversation and why?

Does Pilate say some profound things unwittingly, if so what are they?

What does this conversation teach us about unjust suffering? How can God use it?

Study 9

The first Conversation with the Risen Lord

John 20.1-18

Mary was the first to discover that the tomb was empty; she was the first to have a conversation with the risen Jesus. She had been there at the crucifixion; one of a small circle of women gathered near the cross with Mary the mother of Jesus, her sister, Mary the wife of Clopas and Mary Magdalene (19.25-27). Only John from among the disciples was with them, the rest had fled. So much for the men! Mary Magdalene had watched him die on the cross, and heard his final words joining John and his mother Mary together before crying out, 'It is finished' – literally meaning, 'It is paid!' (19.30). She had watched the whole anguished event: the crucifixion, the mocking, his murmured words of comfort to the soldiers and the thieves, the darkness, his cry of dereliction, his thirst, his final gasping breaths before he gave up his spirit. The entire savage, but solemn, scene was terrible and initially inexplicable until in time the necessity of it, its sacrificial nature as an act of atonement, was laid bare.

As Peter would write later, 'He himself bore our sins in his body on the tree, so that we might die to sins and live for righteousness; by his wounds you have been healed' (1 Peter 2.24). The wounds were visible now for all to see: dying wounds, healing wounds. Perhaps amongst the women only Jesus' mother, Mary, expected it (see Luke 2.35). Now indeed the sword pierced her heart. Mary Magdalene watched him die and saw the signs of death when the spear was thrust into his side (John 19.34). She saw him being taken down from the cross into the custody of Joseph of Arimathea and Nicodemus, who had talked with Jesus by night, and she knew where they had buried him, carefully, generously and lovingly (19.38-42). She had watched his burial (Matthew 27.61) and she was determined to return just as soon as light came, on the first morning after the Sabbath. But sometime on the Sunday night after he had preached in the Spirit to those in bondage in hell (1 Peter 3.19), Jesus was resurrected. He went from one form of existence to another: he was transformed, raised from the dead, the first fruits of a new existence. Resurrection was not simply his own rising from the dead, but the start of a new world order: the kingdom had come!

For Mary it had all started months, possibly years, before. She came from the region of Galilee, from a small West Coast village on the Sea called Magdala. It most probably took its name from an Aramaic word meaning tower or elevation. Perhaps the village was on an elevation beside the sea, a cliff or rocky promontory, or maybe there was a look-out post or tower, clearly visible from the sea to guide sailors back on stormy nights. At any rate, whatever the reason for the name of the village, Mary carried its name into history. She was Mary from Magdala, Mary Magdalene, one of the most well known characters in the New Testament. Life had not been easy for her. We cannot be certain of her background, there is no evidence that she was a prostitute or should be linked with the woman who approached Jesus in the Pharisee Simon's house. That woman who *was* a prostitute bathed Jesus feet with her tears, wiped them with her hair, kissed them and anointed them with perfume (Luke 7.37-38). Such extravagant care or worship resulted from a deep knowledge of forgiveness: she loved much because she was forgiven much, or she loved much and was forgiven much (7.47).

As Jesus said in explaining her behaviour to Simon, who had given Jesus no kiss, no washing or anointing on arrival, this woman did all these things so extravagantly because she loved so much. The one had led to another. But having said all this about the prostitute in Simon's house, there is no certainty that this was necessarily Mary Magdalene, tempting though it might be to join together the Mary clearly described in Luke 8.2 with the story in the preceding chapter. No, what we are clearly told is that by this early stage of Jesus' ministry, Mary called Magdalene, together with other women like Joanna, the wife of an official in Herod, the Tetrarch's court, called Chuza, Susanna, and many other women, all supported Jesus and the Apostles in their ministry. The sole fact we are told about Mary Magdalene is that she had been delivered of seven demons. From what must have been a torrid and tempestuous life, in which these demons held sway, she was delivered and given a new purposeful and peaceful existence. To have been delivered of them was in her case ample grounds for *loving much* as well, which she evidently did thereafter.

Given the lack of information about Mary's early or previous life, her later proximity to Jesus and the speculation about her lifestyle before her deliverance from the demons, it is not surprising that this gap in knowledge has been colourfully elaborated by authors, painters and theologians ever since. In fact legions of legends, myths and traditions have been manufactured about Mary. From Pope Leo the Great's wrong inference that she was a prostitute, artists from the Renaissance onwards have portrayed her as such. Guido Reni represented her repenting from her sinful ways and this representation remained common thereafter.

Mary also featured in several of the Gnostic gospels discovered in a cache at Nag Hammadi by the Nile in Egypt in 1945. In the Gospel of

Philip, Mary is named as Jesus' companion and in the Gospel of Mary (an earlier discovery than the Gnostic gospels at Nag Hammadi), she is portrayed as a disciple with a deeper understanding of Jesus' teaching than the Apostles. Such work is regarded as an expression of an early form of feminism within the church. But all these traditions are without biblical basis and find their final speculative or fictional fantasising in Dan Brown's book *The Da Vinci Code*, where legend has turned into full-blown fantasy. The simple truth about Mary is that she was transformed by Jesus and consequently became one of his most devoted followers, sticking close to him, especially during the Passion and then most famously at the time of his resurrection. That conversation between Mary and Jesus in the Garden near to the tomb is the conversation for which she is justifiably famous and which we now follow.

Mary saw where Jesus was buried (see Matthew 27.61 and Luke 23.55). Matthew says that she watched from opposite the tomb as Jesus was laid to rest. Luke tells us that the women who had watched the burial returned home that evening to prepare spices for his body, even though Nicodemus had brought 75lbs of aloes and myrrh with which to wrap the body in strips of linen cloth on the Friday night (John 19.39-40). At first light on the first day of the week the women returned, while the Apostles were still behind locked doors, frightened and seemingly paralysed by grief (Mark 16.10). The women had been more or less the last to leave on the Friday, and now they were the first to arrive. (The last to leave and the first to arrive – what does that tell us about the women compared to the men?). When they arrived with the spices they found the gravestone rolled away (Matthew 28.2; Mark 16.4; Luke 24.2). They had asked themselves on the way down how they would roll the stone away (Mark 16.3), but astonishingly they found it open and Matthew tells us that this was the work of an earthquake (Matthew 28.2). Next they saw an angel or angels. In Matthew 28.2, this powerful angel sat on the stone that was rolled away from the tomb, terrified the guards and addressed them (28.5). In Mark, the angel is described as being like a 'young man dressed in a white robe' sitting on the side of the tomb (16.5), and in Luke 'two men in clothes that gleamed like lightning' (24.4) also memorably addressed the women by saying, 'Why do you look for the living among the dead? He is not here; he has risen!' (24.5-6) All four gospel writers are quite clear that it was the women who discovered the empty tomb; they saw that the stone was rolled away; they met with the angels and they returned to the Apostles who were in some kind of hiding and they told them what they had seen. The Apostles did not believe what the women said, for which Jesus later rebuked them (Mark 16.11,14; Luke 24.11), but Peter and John had enough sense to check it out for themselves. They ran to the tomb. Mary Magdalene had, it seems, also returned to the garden with the two disciples, Peter and John. She lingered in the garden trying to piece it all together and waited to re-enter the tomb after Peter and John returned to tell the rest of the disciples of their discovery. It was then that she became the first witness to the resurrection and had the first conversation with the risen lord.

After Peter and John had left the tomb (20.10) Mary went back, for it had a kind of magnetic attraction for her. She stood outside crying. All the pent up emotion of the past few days came pouring out. It seemed like the final indignity. The body of Jesus taken! She peered into the tomb once more; again she saw two angels in white (Mark 16.5 & Luke 24.2). They were seated where the body of Jesus had been, 'one at the head and the other at the foot' (20.12). They asked her, 'Woman, why are you crying?' She replied, 'They have taken my Lord away and I don't know where they have put him' (20.13). Presumably she thought either the authorities or grave robbers had seized his body. She turned to look around the garden for some clue as to the body's whereabouts and at that moment she saw Jesus and instantly assumed that he was the gardener. He asked the same question, 'Why are you crying? Who is it you are looking for?' She wanted to know where the body was so that she might go and get it and return it to the proper resting place. In her grief and confusion she did not register the words of the angels; she did not recognise Jesus either, perhaps because she was kept from recognising him, or perhaps because in some way he was still hidden from her. But all that changed when he addressed her by name.

He called her in a familiar way. Was it the sound of his voice? Was it the way he pronounced it? Was it simply a moment of revelation? Was it a combination of all or several of these? There is no doubt that just as hearing is the last sense to go in a dying person, so hearing – maybe more than sight – prompts the memory or recall more than the other senses. At any rate, when Jesus said her name, all her weeping, all her foreboding and all her grief were instantly transformed. No wonder she instinctively cried 'Rabboni' and held onto him, grasping him to make sure that he was real and embracing him in her relief, love and joy. But Jesus had changed. Why should she *not* hold him, as he had *not* yet returned to his Father? Was it because his status had changed and now, as the resurrected Lord, he was less approachable? Or was it an encouragement to get on with the task of making known his resurrection to the disciples who had as yet not seen him without any delay? Or was it that in his resurrected body he could not be restricted by human need? Or was it something else? At any rate, Mary was given both a privilege and a responsibility. She was chosen to be the first witness to the resurrection. She must now 'go and tell' that Jesus was alive and that he was 'returning to his Father and their Father and to my God and your God' (20.17). She went straightaway to them and said plainly, and no doubt with exultant joy, 'I have seen the Lord' (20.18).

Study Questions

Do you have a timetable in your mind of what happened that first Easter Day? Would anyone care to share their *rough guide* to Easter day?

If you had been inside the tomb at the moment of resurrection taking a photograph, what would you have seen?

Was the stone rolled away to let Jesus out or to let the disciples in?

What was the role of the angels? What did Mary think had happened to the body of Jesus?

Why do you think Mary Magdalene did not recognise Jesus?

Why was the use of Mary's name by Jesus so crucial in Mary's recognition of him? In what other moments can the voice be especially important?

Is the significance of the resurrection more than Jesus overcoming death?

What is the duty of a witness? What news do we have to share?

What was special about Mary Magdalene?

Study 10

A Conversation on the beach about restoration

John 21.1-25

We have come to our last conversation with Jesus taken from John's gospel. Jesus' conversations have been diverse, ranging from one with the Roman Governor whilst awaiting crucifixion to one with his mother at the happy event of a wedding; from one with a woman caught in adultery to one with a ruler of the Jews. They have taken place in very different settings: at a wedding, by a well, at night in Jerusalem, in a Roman palace, in a cemetery garden by a tomb, and now finally on a beach on the shore of Lake Galilee. This is the final conversation of the gospel and occupies most of the last chapter. It is a conversation full of reality, hope, some pain, but is entirely necessary to the mission of the church thereafter. It is a conversation that gives hope to all of us who fail, who long to return to our former relationship with God or Christ, and begin our lives again. The possibility of forgiveness and a fresh start is one of the sweetest gifts of grace; it is literally like water to a dying man. It can revive, restore and re-invigorate someone in their life like nothing else.

This week our national newspapers have been full of the fall from office of a highly placed political couple in national life. Their fall has been tragic and has involved lying, deception, ambition, adultery, jealousy, revenge, breakdown of family relationships, imprisonment, resignation, and loss of reputation. It could not have been more tragic for all concerned. It was failure on an epic scale and would have been compelling theatre in the hands of the bard. But nonetheless, the grace of God can bring restoration if we give him all the pieces. He cannot erase the past or alter the record, but he can restore hope, give strength and forgive guilt. It is interesting that the final conversation in the gospel is the message of forgiveness and hope, which is the central theme of the gospel. It is the gospel in the gospel. Or in other words it is the message in the story.

The story behind this final conversation is well known. It revolves around Peter – the leading Apostle, the rock: forthright, headstrong, reckless and impetuous. He swore that he would never desert his leader, Jesus. Luke tells us Jesus said, 'Simon, Simon, Satan has asked to sift you as wheat. But I have prayed for you, Simon, that your faith may not fail. And when you have turned back, strengthen your brothers.' But Simon replied, 'Lord, I am ready to go with you to prison and to death.' Jesus answered, 'I tell you, Peter, before the cock crows today, you will deny three times that you know me' (Luke 22.31-34). Peter did not pray in Gethsemane. He was not ready for what would follow. He tried to prevent Jesus' arrest by using his sword and cutting off the ear of the High Priest's servant Malchus (John 18.10). He followed the arrested Jesus into the High Priest's house, gaining admittance through John (18.16), where he proceeded to deny Jesus three times (18.17ff). On the third occasion the cock crowed and Luke tells us that Jesus turned and looked directly at Peter (Luke 22.61-62).

He went out and wept bitterly. It must have been the lowest point of

Peter's life; all that bravado and bluster amounted to nothing, indeed worse than nothing. Most of us have moments when we do the very thing we don't want to do, or don't do the very thing we should do. Through unpreparedness, fear and weakness we fail. Afterwards we feel remorse, guilt and a kind of inner paralysis that depresses and restricts us. For Peter, events must have moved so swiftly to Jesus' crucifixion and death. He may have thought that his own self-respect and hopefulness were buried with Jesus on the Friday night. News of the empty tomb on the morning of the first day of the week must have brought a glimmer of hope. He ran down with John and saw it for himself, and the evening of that same day he saw Jesus alive. He was no doubt overjoyed, but as yet he had had no conversation with him. There was unfinished business that would come out later, on the shore of Galilee.

The prelude to the conversation was well stage-managed. In one sense the first 14 verses of the chapter are the backcloth to the conversation. As Jesus told the disciples earlier, they were to go to Galilee where they were to meet him (see Mark 16.7). Whether in obedience to that command or out of despondency, thinking that their task had come prematurely to an end with Jesus' crucifixion and not knowing what to make of the resurrection, they went back to Galilee where they were mostly from. It was safer there than in Jerusalem, and maybe they anticipated further instructions. At the suggestion of Peter they went fishing (21.3). Presumably waiting around for something to happen was more than Peter could bear and, ever active, he wanted to do something to occupy his racing and disturbed thoughts. The events of the crucifixion, the guilt of his own denial, the mystery of the resurrection and what it meant, and the uncertainty about the future must have weighed heavily upon him. To be outdoors and doing what he was used to doing in familiar surroundings may have been some consolation, even if it meant a sleepless night and no catch. The words 'they caught nothing' (21.3) resonate with others in the gospel, for example: 'They have no more wine' (2.3); 'Apart from me you can do nothing' (15.5): and there was also the residual memory that on the night before his call Peter had also caught nothing!

They must have been wearily hauling in the nets and making for home when early in the morning they saw a stranger on the shore. He called out to them. They were only about a hundred yards from the shore (21.8), definitely within shouting distance. 'Friends, haven't you any fish?' It was not so much a question as a statement: you haven't any fish. They said 'No.' He instructed them to throw the net on the right side of the boat, and immediately they could feel the tug of fish, not just a few tiddlers, but a mass of large writhing, healthy fish, the like of which you normally only catch in deep water – not there, so close to the shore.

Just as the disciples with Jesus at Emmaus recognised him only when he broke bread (Luke 24.31), here the familiarity of the words and actions gave his identity away, even as their eyes were mysteriously kept from recognising him (Luke 24.16). Now this extraordinary catch was a repeat of only one other like it in their lives (see Luke 5.1-11). It was enough to convince John that the stranger was Jesus. Leaping out of the boat, first John, and then Peter making himself decent (21.7), made for the shore and Jesus. There was already a fire lit. There was already bread and fish to eat. (How did he get them?) Breakfast was ready and prepared, and to fill out the feast he asked them to bring over some of their catch, which by then had been brought to shore by the other disciples (21.8). Simon Peter went back to help bring the fish. They counted them. There were 153 of them; none of them were small and the net was not torn.

The catch was the final miracle or sign of the gospel. The epilogue is not one of the seven signs pointing to the divinity of Christ so much as part of Jesus' final commission to the disciples. It was a commission to catch not fish but people, a commission that was dependent on his dynamic instruction and the disciples' dependence on him. It was a commission in which he would sustain the disciples, providing for them, nurturing them and attending to their needs. Finally it was a commission that would be ultimately successful. All this was conveyed by this miracle, a kind of epilogue to the gospel and a foretaste of the future.

But now it was time for breakfast. Jesus acted as host, distributing the bread and fish. Once again he *took* and he *gave*; and they ate. It was a quiet breakfast it seems; no one asked him anything (21.12) – what would you say? And Peter, perhaps anxiously, awaited the conversation that was bound to happen – he didn't have to wait long!

It is likely that after breakfast they moved away from the fire where they had been cooking the fish, for later we are told that 'Peter turned and saw that the disciple whom Jesus loved was following them'(21.20). Alone, but perhaps overheard by John, who recorded what he would have regarded as a significant conversation, Jesus and Peter talked. Jesus was not slow in coming to the point. He addressed Peter formally, calling him 'Simon, son of John' thereby giving him his full birth name and not including his own pet name for Simon, which as we all know is Peter, meaning a rock. Here Jesus was addressing the very core of his identity. His time in the High Priest's courtyard, when he denied the Lord three times, had been most un rock-like. So it was Simon, son of John now, and the question also went to the heart of the matter, 'Do you love me?' Not, 'Do you regret what you did?' or 'Please will you explain yourself' or 'What came over you?' or even, 'I told you so,' all of which would have been more or less recriminatory and sterile questions. No, Jesus asked the only question that mattered as far as he was concerned, the only motivating fruitful question that can be asked after someone has fallen spiritually, 'Do you love me?' In fact that wasn't the question exactly. It was, 'Do you love me *more* than these?' (That is, the other disciples presumably.) It was a comparative question; not only was he asked *whether* he loved (*agape*) Jesus, but he was asked whether he loved him *more* than these. Why did Jesus frame the question in such a way? The reply ran the risk of someone claiming greater love than others who were already good friends and who knew him and his strengths and weaknesses well, and especially after such a signal failure.

Perhaps Jesus framed the question in such a way because it made Peter dig deeper in his reply, but more especially since he was going to need a deep, even deeper love, because the demands upon him would be greater than on the others. After all, he would have to lead the early church, at least until the Apostle Paul arrived on the scene many years later. A deeper love for a deeper service and that it is what Jesus had in mind. On Peter's admission of his love (*philia* – friendship love), Jesus commanded him to feed his lambs or sheep. In other words love for Christ was to be expressed in love for his body, love for his sheep, and love for his church. Three times Peter was asked the same question and on the third occasion he was *hurt* (21.17). It was painful. But it was meant to be, for Jesus was cauterising a wound. He was overlaying in these three questions and their positive response the three denials Peter had previously made. It was like spiritual surgery: cleansing, re-affirming and restoring and above all forgiving, yet at the same time preparing Peter for his future ministry of endless giving and sacrifice.

So Jesus seamlessly continued: 'When you are old you will stretch out your hands, and someone else will dress you and lead you where you do not want to go' (20.18). And John commented for clarification that Jesus was speaking about Peter's death, which like that of his Lord, would be by crucifixion (although tradition has it that he was crucified upside down, feeling unworthy of being crucified in the same way as Jesus). As to Peter's enquiry about what would happen to John (20.21), Peter was bluntly told not to worry about him, but instead to concentrate on his own following of Jesus. This serves as a reminder to us that each person is given their own ministry or calling and it is not our business to wonder why it is not like another's, but to get on with what we have been given to do. Jesus' final instruction in the conversation to Peter was to follow him (20.22).

How must Peter have felt following this conversation? Affirmed, restored, and relieved? Yes, all of that; and much more. He was re-commissioned, he was charged with a task, he was energised for the future. In just a few weeks' time, on the day of Pentecost, he would stand up and preach to the wondering crowds and 3,000 would believe (Acts 2.41). His love for Jesus was working out in caring for this new church formed in Jerusalem that day.

Study Questions

What kind of mixture of emotions must have Peter felt at the time of the Resurrection?

What kind of memories would the catch of fish have brought to mind?

What do you think the atmosphere would have been at the breakfast on the beach?

What lessons were John or Jesus seeking to convey in this story of the catch?

Why did Jesus ask the question 'do you love me' three times?

What would you say was at the core of this conversation?

What does love for Jesus feel like? How can it grow?

How was Peter to show his love for Jesus?

Why was it so important to have this conversation?

What is the effect on people of some kind of failure whether moral, professional (i.e. something that goes wrong at work) or relational?

Is there anyone we should be having a conversation with?

How do you think Peter would have been feeling and thinking at the end of this conversation?

What is your impression of Jesus in this conversation?

Which of all the conversations we have studied means the most to you and why?

A Meditation

on some of the sentences we have heard in these studies

This meditation or prayer time could be used towards the end of this course, or simply on the final night. It could be accompanied by worship, a simple breaking of bread or communion, a lighted candle and music during which these sentences are read out slowly with plenty of time in between so that they resonate with the group. After a pause at the end there could be a time of open prayer or communion. It could be a fitting conclusion to the whole series, and if used in Advent or Lent, a preparation for Christmas or Easter.

Here are some quotations from the passages we have studied which can be read slowly as part of the meditation:

'The word became flesh and made his dwelling among us. We have seen his glory, the glory of the One and Only, who came from the Father, full of grace and truth' (1.14).

'They have no more wine' (2.3).

'I tell you the truth, no one can see the Kingdom of God unless he is born again' (3.3).

'I tell you the truth; no one can enter the Kingdom of God unless he is born of water and the Spirit. Flesh gives birth to flesh, Spirit gives birth to spirit' (3.5).

'Everyone who drinks this water will thirst again, but whoever drinks the water I give him will never thirst. Indeed, the water I give him will become in him a spring of water welling up to eternal life.' (4.14)

'Go call your husband and come back' (4.16).

'I have no husband, she replied' (4.17).

'Come see a man who told me everything I ever did. Could this be the Christ?' (4.29)

'I have food to eat that you know nothing about' (4.32).

'If any of you is without sin, let him be the first to throw a stone at you' (8.7).

'Has no one condemned you...Then neither do I condemn you. Go now, and leave your life of sin' (8.10-11).

'Our friend Lazarus has fallen asleep but I have gone to wake him' (11.11).

'Lord, if you had been here my brother would not have died. But I know that even now God will give you whatever you ask' (11.22).

'I am the resurrection and the life. He who believes in me will live even though he dies; and whoever lives and believes in me will never die. Do you believe this?' (11.25-26).

'Where have you laid him? Come and see, Lord. Jesus wept' (11.34-35).

'Lazarus, come out. Take off the grave clothes and let him go' (11.43-44).

'Then Pilate went back inside the palace and summoned Jesus and asked him, 'are you the king of the Jews?'' (18.33)

'Is that your own idea or did others talk to you about me?' (18.33b-34).

'My kingdom is not of this world' (18.36).

'"You are a king then!" Pilate asked. Jesus answered, "You are right in saying I am a king. In fact, for this reason, I was born and for this I came into the world, to testify to the truth. Everyone on the side of truth listens to me"' (18.37).

'"What is truth?" Pilate asked' (18.37-38a).

'Then Pilate took Jesus and had him flogged. The soldiers twisted together a crown of thorns and put it on his head. They clothed him in a purple robe and went up to him again and again, saying: "Hail King of the Jews!" And they struck him in the face.' (19.1-2)

'"Here is your King, Pilate said to the Jews. But they shouted, "Take him away! Take him away! Crucify him!"' (19.14-15)

Silence

****

'Mary stood outside the tomb crying. As she wept, she bent over to look into the tomb and saw two angels in white, seated where Jesus body had been one at the head and other at the foot. They asked her '"why are you crying?"' (20.11-13)

'She turned round and saw Jesus standing there, but did not realise that it was Jesus. "Woman" he said, "why are you crying? Who is it you are looking for?"' (20.14)

'Jesus said to her, "Mary"' (20.16).

'Do not hold onto me, for I have not yet returned to the Father. Go instead to my brothers and tell them, "I am returning to my Father and your Father, to my God and your God."' (20.17)

Silence

****

'So they went out and got into the boat, but that night they caught nothing' (21.3b).

'"Throw your net on the right side of the boat and you will find some.2 When they did, they were unable to haul the net in because of the large number of fish' (21.6).

'Then the disciple whom Jesus loved said to Peter, "It is the Lord"'(21.7).

'Jesus came, took the bread and gave it to them, and did the same with the fish' (21.13).

'When they had finished eating, Jesus said to Simon Peter, "Simon son of John, do you truly love me more than these?" "Yes Lord," he said "you know that I love you"' (21.15).

'Jesus said, "Feed my lambs"' (21.15).

'The third time he said to him, "Simon, son of John, do you love me?" Peter was hurt.' (21.17)

'When Peter turned and saw the disciple whom Jesus loved was following them... he asked "what about him?"' (21.20-21)

'Jesus answered, "If I want him to remain alive until I return, what is that to you? You must follow me"' (21.22).

Silence

****

For further reading

***The Word from the Throne* – Patrick Whitworth** (Holy Printing 2011). A fresh survey of common themes from John's writings. Patrick offers seven couplets or paradoxes taken from John's writings, all of which challenge the Church today. 'A book which will bring comfort, hope and strength for the journey ahead' – Charles Marnham
For other books by Patrick Whitworth visit patrickwhitworth.co.uk. Patrick also offers day courses based on his books.

***The Wild Gospel* – Alison Morgan** (3rd printing Monarch 2009). A personal and challenging look at the ministry of Jesus, the ministry of the Church and the experience of faith today. 'A ground-breaking, exciting and moving book that could not be more timely as the Church looks for fresh ways of speaking God's truth in and to our culture' - Rowan Williams. For other books by Alison Morgan visit resource-arm.net.

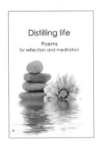

***Distilling Life* – poems for reflection and meditation** (ReSource 2011). A collection of poetry edited by Martin Cavender and Alison Morgan. Ranging over 26 centuries, the poems have been carefully selected and arranged in such a way as to take the reader on a spiritual journey. With illustrations to help unleash the imagination, this is a unique collection.

ReSource is a registered Church of England charity based in Wells, Somerset. We work all over the UK and beyond, supporting the local church and publishing a range of books and course materials to strengthen the mission and ministry of the Church, along with a termly full colour topical magazine. To find out more about our publications, or to explore our range of day programmes please visit our website or contact the office.

ReSource : www.resource-arm.net
Email : office@resource-arm.net